Ranger Rick's NatureScope

BIRDS, BIRDS, BIRDS!

National Wildlife Federation

Chelsea House Publishers
Philadelphia

This Chelsea House edition of NatureScope® with permission of Learning Triangle Press, an imprint of McGraw-Hill.

First published in hardback edition ©1998 Chelsea House Publishers.

Library of Congress Cataloging-in-Publication Data

Birds, birds, birds / National Wildlife Federation.
    p. cm. — (Ranger Rick's naturescope)
    Originally published: New York : McGraw-Hill, 1989.
    Includes bibliographical references (p.) and index.
    ISBN 0-7910-4830-6 (hc)
    1. Birds—Study and teaching—Activity programs. 2. Birds—Study
and teaching (Elementary)   I. National Wildlife Federation.
II. Series.
    [QL677.5.B485 1998]
    372.3'57—dc21

        97-51931
        CIP

NatureScope® was originally conceived by National Wildlife Federation's School Programs Editorial Staff, under the direction of Judy Braus, Editor. Special thanks to all of the Editorial Staff, Scientific, Educational Consultants and Contributors who brought this series of eighteen publications to life.

Other Titles in Ranger Rick's NatureScope

AMAZING MAMMALS, PART I
AMAZING MAMMALS, PART II
ASTRONOMY ADVENTURES
BIRDS, BIRDS, BIRDS
DIGGING INTO DINOSAURS
DISCOVERING DESERTS
DIVING INTO OCEANS
GEOLOGY: THE ACTIVE EARTH
INCREDIBLE INSECTS

LETS HEAR IT FOR HERPS:
ALL ABOUT AMPHIBIANS AND REPTILES
POLLUTION: PROBLEMS & SOLUTIONS
RAIN FORESTS: TROPICAL TREASURES
TREES ARE TERRIFIC!
WADING INTO WETLANDS
WILD ABOUT WEATHER
WILD & CRAFTY

A Close-Up Look At Birds, Birds, Birds!

L looking at the Table of Contents, you can see we've divided *Birds, Birds, Birds!* into five chapters (each of which deals with a broad bird theme), a craft section, and an appendix. Each of the five chapters includes *background information* that explains concepts and vocabulary, *activities* that relate to the chapter theme, and *Copycat Pages* that reinforce many of the concepts introduced in the activities.

You can choose single activity ideas or teach each chapter as a unit. Either way, each activity stands by itself and includes teaching objectives, a list of materials needed, suggested age groups, subjects covered, and a step-by-step explanation of how to do the activity. (The objectives, materials, age groups, and subjects are highlighted in the left-hand margin for easy reference.)

Age Groups

The suggested age groups are:

- Primary (grades K-2)
- Intermediate (grades 3-5)
- Advanced (grades 6-8)

Each chapter begins with primary activities and ends with intermediate or advanced activities. But don't feel bound by the grade levels we suggest. You'll be able to adapt many of the activities to fit your particular age group and needs.

Outdoor Activities

There's no better way to study birds than to go outside and watch them. We've included several outdoor activities in this issue. These are coded in the chapters in which they appear with this symbol:

Copycat Pages

The *Copycat Pages* supplement the activities and include ready-to-copy games, puzzles, coloring pages, worksheets, and mazes. *Answers to all Copycat Pages are on the inside back cover.*

What's At The End

The sixth section, *Crafty Corner,* will give you some art and craft ideas that complement many of the activities in the first five chapters. And the last section, the *Appendix,* is loaded with reference suggestions that include books, films, and bird activity sources. The Appendix also has bird questions and answers, a bird glossary, and suggestions for where to go for more bird information.

Fitting It All In

We've tried to combine the science activities in *Birds, Birds, Birds!* with language arts, history, creative writing, geography, math, social studies, and art activities to make this booklet as versatile as possible. If you plan to do an entire unit on birds, *Birds, Birds, Birds!* can be your major source of background information and activity ideas. But if you have time to use only a few of the activities, check the objectives and subjects to see which ones will complement what you're already doing.

We hope *Birds, Birds, Birds!* will provide a source of activity ideas and project suggestions that you can use over and over again with your groups.

Protecting Nests And Feathers

In several of the activities we suggest that you bring in samples of feathers. In the United States and Canada it is illegal to collect most feathers found in the wild. (It's OK to take starling, pigeon, and house sparrow feathers in every state and province. Check with your state or provincial wildlife agency to learn about rules concerning game bird feathers and to find out about special educational permits.) You can ask for feathers at poultry farms and zoos, but even at zoos, you're not allowed to take feathers of endangered or native species. The rules about collecting feathers also apply to collecting eggs, dead birds, and nests—even abandoned ones.

Although these laws may seem strict or even silly, there are good reasons for them. Before the laws were passed, people would shoot birds to collect their feathers. If someone was caught with feathers of a rare or endangered bird, he or she could just say that the feathers were found on the ground—and there was no way to prove guilt. People would also collect nests and sometimes even eggs. Although these laws are very difficult to enforce, they at least can offer more protection than was provided before the laws were passed.

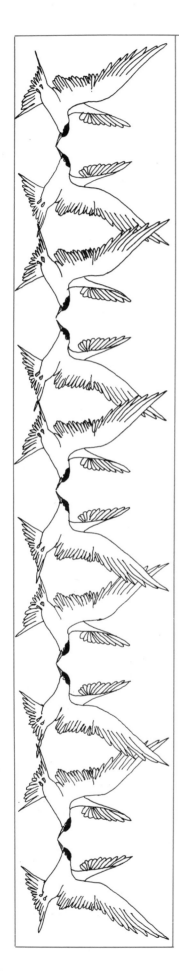

WHAT MAKES A BIRD A BIRD?

t may be hard to believe that a 300-pound (135-kg) ostrich galloping across the African grasslands has much in common with a wasp-sized hummingbird hovering in front of a flower. But all birds, even those as different as an ostrich and a hummingbird, share many characteristics.

Birds belong to a large group of animals called *vertebrates* (animals with backbones) and they make up a special group (class) of the vertebrates called *Aves*. (*Aves* is the Latin word for bird and it is the root of bird words such as avian and aviary.) Fish, amphibians, reptiles, and mammals are examples of other classes of vertebrates.

Reptilian Relatives: You might not think reptiles such as turtles, crocodiles, and lizards have much in common with birds, but they do. About 160 million years ago, birds evolved from ancient reptiles, keeping many reptilian characteristics. (Many scientists think birds evolved from small dinosaurlike reptiles.) For example, both birds and reptiles lay eggs, have partially hollow bones, have similar types of skulls and ear bones, and have scales covering parts of their bodies.

But as birds evolved, they also became very different from reptiles. Many of the scales that covered their bodies became flatter and longer, evolving into *feathers*. Birds also developed horny beaks but kept reptilelike scales on their legs and feet. In addition, their forelimbs gradually evolved into wings.

Here's a closer look at some of the characteristics that make a bird a bird:

Feathers: All birds grow feathers, making birds different from all other animals. Birds have several different types of feathers, from stiff *contour* feathers, which cover the wings and body, to fluffy *down* feathers, which help insulate a bird and keep it warm. The most common type is the contour feather. Contour feathers are very strong but also very lightweight. The stem, or *shaft,* is a hollow tube made of a very hard material called *keratin.* (Keratin is the same material that a reptile's scales and our fingernails are made of.) The contour feathers are stiff but flexible and help streamline a bird to give it a smooth, sleek shape. And the special contour feathers on the wings, called the flight feathers, are shaped to fan the air, creating "lift" which helps a bird get off the ground, maneuver in the air, and land safely.

Feathers grow much the way our hair grows. The base of each shaft is rooted in a tiny follicle in the skin and receives an ongoing supply of nutrients from the blood. When the feather is fully grown, the base of the shaft closes and the feather dies. Eventually it will fall out or be pushed out by a new feather that grows in the same follicle.

Besides helping birds fly, feathers help protect a bird's sensitive skin, just as hair helps protect a mammal's skin. Some feathers are also great insulators because they trap a bird's body heat. This insulation is one reason that birds can live in Antarctica and in other very cold places. Feathers also form brightly colored crests and tail displays, which are important in courtship behavior. (See page 13 for more about feathers.)

Winging It: All birds have wings—even ostriches, penguins, and other flightless birds. The wings of a bird are attached to chest muscles called the *pectoral* or flight muscles. In flying birds, the pectorals are very powerful muscles. (The breast meat on a chicken, turkey, or other bird is the bird's pectoral muscle.)

Bird wings are streamlined like an airplane's wings and zip through the air easily. The wings are curved on top (convex) and are flat or slightly curved (concave) on

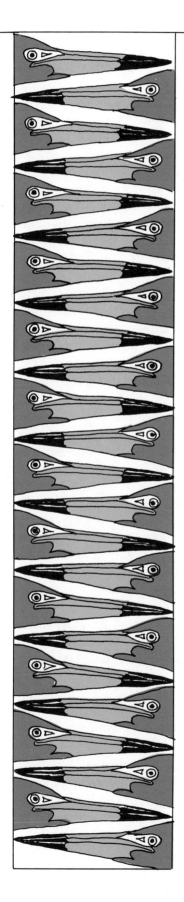

the bottom. This special shape gives a flying bird the *lift* it needs to get off the ground. And once a bird takes off, the outer ends of the wings (where the main flight feathers attach) act like propellers and rudders, helping the bird move up, down, and forward through the air.

The type of flying a bird does depends on the size and shape of its wings. For example, large soaring birds such as eagles and vultures have long, broad wings. Forest birds such as some owls and songbirds have short, broad wings for flying in and out of thick vegetation. And birds that are fast fliers and spend a lot of time flying, such as falcons and swifts, have long pointed wings.

Wings are important even to flightless birds. Penguins use their wings as flippers to help them swim underwater. And wings help ostriches keep their balance as they gallop across the grasslands.

Boning Up on Birds: Even though it doesn't weigh much, a bird's skeleton is very strong. Many of the bones in a bird's skeleton are *fused,* or joined together. This gives the skeleton extra strength. Most of a bird's bones are hollow or partially hollow, and some have very thin braces of bone inside for support. (Mammals have thicker, denser, heavier bones.)

Having a very strong but lightweight frame is important because it allows birds to be light enough to get off the ground and stay in the air but gives them the strength needed to support their large flight muscles and protect their internal organs.

A Bird's Eye View: Most birds can see much better than other animals, including people. They have very large eyes that can focus sharply on both nearby and faraway objects. And unlike many mammals, they can see color. Birds use their keen eyesight to find food, keep an eye on enemies, spot mates, and find a place to live.

Birds' eyes, which in most birds are located on the sides of the head, can focus independently of each other so that a bird can see two different images at the same time. This is called *monocular* vision. But when they focus straight ahead, birds have *binocular* vision, with both eyes focusing on the same image. Some birds, such as owls, have binocular vision most of the time because their eyes face forward, just as people's do. (Binocular vision allows an animal to judge distance, making it easier to follow movement, such as when an owl follows a running mouse. Monocular vision gives an animal a wider field of vision.)

Even though birds can focus each eye independently of the other, their eyes are relatively fixed in their sockets so that they can't roll their eyes around the way we can. Instead, birds have to turn their heads to see in different directions. That's why you often see birds twisting and cocking their heads. Some owls can twist their heads more than three-fourths of a full circle!

Holes in the Head: Most birds have a very keen sense of hearing. Their ears are located on each side of the head, just below and in back of the eyes. You usually can't see the ears though, because in most birds they are just small holes covered with feathers. The holes lead to the middle and inner ears, which are very sensitive to both high and low-pitched sounds. Birds depend on their sense of hearing to find their prey, to find mates, and to detect danger. Owls and other night-flying birds often have especially good hearing and can detect mice squeaking and leaves rustling from far away.

5

Big on Beaks: Each type of bird has a different type of beak, depending on the kind of food it eats. (See page 29 for more about beaks and food.) Birds use their beaks mainly to gather food and drink water. (Many birds also use their beaks to tear their food into pieces they can swallow.) But birds also use their beaks to collect nesting materials, preen their feathers (see page 41), scratch their bodies, attack enemies, caress their mates, and feed their young.

Smelling Like a Bird: Most birds seem to have a poorly developed sense of smell and rely on their keen senses of sight and hearing to find food and avoid predators. But scientists think that turkey vultures, kiwis, and a few other birds do sniff out their food as well as use their other senses.

Tricky Tongues: Bird tongues come in all shapes and sizes. And birds use their tongues in many different ways—to taste, spear, hold, and tear food.

Warm-blooded Birds: All birds are warm-blooded, just as mammals are, which means they maintain a constant body temperature even if the temperature around them changes. (Cold-blooded animals, such as reptiles, fish, and amphibians, can control their body temperatures only by moving to warmer or cooler areas.)

A Special Gland: Most birds have a special oil gland located just above the base of the tail. The oil gland secretes oil that the bird rubs over its feathers with its beak. The oil helps condition and clean the feathers and in some birds helps make the feathers water-repellent. Scientists also think the oil has special vitamins that are absorbed into the skin and help some birds stay healthy.

Take a Deep Breath: Birds have a very efficient breathing system. They have two lungs, with special balloonlike *air sacs* attached to each one. (Mammals also have two lungs, but they do not have air sacs.) The air sacs spread into different parts of a bird's body, including the hollow parts of the larger bones. They allow a bird to store up more air, push more air through the lungs, and bring more oxygen to the cells. (Birds need a lot of oxygen to help turn the food in their cells into the extra energy they need to fly and maintain a high body temperature.)

Air sacs may also help birds cool down if they get overheated and help some swimming birds stay afloat.

Keeping Cool: Birds do not sweat to cool off, as people and many other mammals do. (They don't have sweat glands.) Instead, many birds pant, breathing in and out very quickly in much the same way that a dog pants. Panting cools the bird as water from the lungs, throat, mouth, and other parts of the body evaporates. Birds also keep cool by taking a bath or sitting in the shade.

Store It in the Crop: When food is swallowed, the muscles in a bird's esophagus push the food down the throat. In many birds, the bottom of the esophagus forms a large sac called the *crop*. The crop stores undigested food before it enters the stomach. Birds that have a crop can gorge when they find a good food source, store the food in the crop, and then slowly digest it later.

Teeth in the Stomach: Food passes from the crop or esophagus into the stomach, where strong stomach acids are secreted to help digest the food chemically. Then the partially digested food passes into the gizzard, which is the specialized muscular part of the stomach. (Most birds have a gizzard, but it is more highly developed in seed-eating birds and birds that eat hard-to-digest food.)

Birds use their gizzards as other animals use their teeth—to grind and crush hard nuts, seeds, grain, and other foods. (Birds do not have teeth.) Many seed-eating birds swallow small stones and grit that help the gizzard grind. (In owls, hawks, and some other birds, anything that can't be broken down in the stomach, such as feathers, fur, or bones, is stored in the gizzard and regurgitated as pellets.)

Flappers

Match the wingbeats of different birds by flapping your arms.

Objectives:
Describe three different types of bird flight. Explain why some birds have fast wingbeats and others have slower wingbeats.

Ages:
Primary and Intermediate

Materials:
- *watch or clock that shows seconds*
- *copies of page 16*
- *scissors*
- *8 index cards per person*
- *chalkboard or large piece of easel paper*
- *markers*

Subjects:
Science, Math, and Crafts

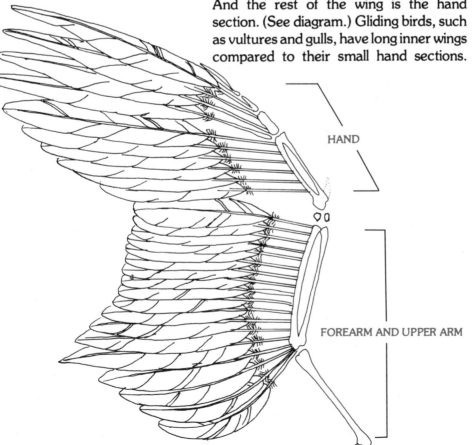

HAND

FOREARM AND UPPER ARM

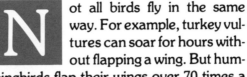ot all birds fly in the same way. For example, turkey vultures can soar for hours without flapping a wing. But hummingbirds flap their wings over 70 times a second as they hover, fly forward, or even fly backward. In this activity, your group can find out how different kinds of birds fly. They can compare their arms to the wings of a bird and see if they can "flap" as fast as a bird can.

First have everyone hold their arms straight out. Explain that a bird's wing is similar to our arm. Both have an upper arm bone connected to the shoulder, an elbow that connects the upper arm to the forearm, and a wrist that connects the forearm to the hand. A bird's hand section is a little different from ours. It has a bony thumb stuck off to one side and two fingerlike bones on the end. (Because a bird's wing is covered with feathers, it's hard to see all the bones. If possible, take a trip to a natural history museum or nature center to look at a bird skeleton.) The upper arm and forearm make up a bird's inner wing. And the rest of the wing is the hand section. (See diagram.) Gliding birds, such as vultures and gulls, have long inner wings compared to their small hand sections.

The large inner wing provides the lift they need to soar. But flapping birds, such as peregrine falcons, have small inner wings and long hand sections. The hand acts like a propeller and pulls the bird forward as it flaps.

Have your kids try out their "wings" by extending their arms and flapping away. See how long they can keep up an easy flapping pace (one flap per second) before they get tired. Then tell them that some birds, such as the lesser golden plover, can fly for 48 hours straight, flapping the whole time. Ask if their arms ache a little bit from flapping. (They should complain that their outer chest muscles—the pectorals—and their arm muscles are tired.) Explain that since we get around by walking, our leg muscles are more fully developed than our chest muscles. But for most birds, it's just the opposite. Their chest muscles are very well developed to power the wings, and their leg muscles are weaker. (Turkeys, chickens, ostriches, and other walking birds have well-developed leg muscles.)

To compare the different wingbeats of birds, copy the chart onto a chalkboard or large piece of easel paper. Ask the kids to decide which rate of flapping they think they can keep up with. For younger children, have the whole group come up and flap together, starting with 20 flaps every 10 seconds to imitate a crow. Then try a robin and a pigeon. By the time you get to starlings, the kids will find it's impossible to keep up.

For older groups, divide into pairs and have one person keep time while the other person flaps.

THE WINGBEAT CHART

Bird	Wingbeat/10 seconds
Crow	20
Robin	23
Pigeon	30
Starling	45
Chickadee	270
Hummingbird	700

(continued next page)

BRANCHING OUT: MATH

Have your group use the wingbeat chart to solve these math problems:

1. Which of these combinations would "make the most flaps"?
   - a hummingbird flapping for 45 seconds
   - ten crows flapping for 65 seconds
   - four starlings flapping for 5 minutes
   - a pigeon, chickadee, and robin flapping for 3 minutes
   - sixteen starlings flapping for 1 minute

   Answer: a pigeon, chickadee, and robin flapping for 3 minutes (5814 flaps)

2. If a crow, robin, pigeon, and starling each flew in the same direction going 30 miles (48 km) per hour, how many times would each one flap if:
   - the crow flew 15 miles
   - the robin flew 45 miles
   - the pigeon flew 90 miles
   - the starling flew 3 miles

   Answers: crow—3600
   robin—12,420
   pigeon—32,400
   starling—1620

3. If a crow, robin, pigeon, starling, chickadee, and hummingbird each flapped their wings for 20 seconds, how many total flaps would there be?
   Answer: 2176 flaps

4. How many wingbeats would you get in one minute from:
   - a hummingbird
   - a chickadee
   - a pigeon

   Answers: hummingbird—4200, chickadee—1620, pigeon—180

BRANCHING OUT: CRAFTS

After the flapping exercise, give each person index cards (3 x 5") and a copy of page 16. Then have the kids make their own flapping motion picture cartoons. Here's how:

1. Cut the index cards in half to make 16 smaller cards. (Each card should be exactly the same size, so tell the kids to measure.)
2. Cut out the pictures and glue each one to the bottom right-hand corner of each card. (Keep the pictures in the order they appear on the sheet.)
3. Arrange the cards one on top of the other, starting with picture #16 on the bottom and ending with picture #1 on top. Staple them together across the side, as shown.
4. Flip through the cards and make your birds "fly."

Staple Here

Super Birds

Discuss the biggest, the tallest, the smallest, and the fastest birds, as well as other bird statistics.

Objectives:
Compare bird sizes and skills. Describe three bird record holders.

Ages:
Primary and Intermediate

In this activity your group can find out some neat "bird statistics" as well as get a feel for how diverse birds are. They will also realize that even though birds are very different, they all share many characteristics.

Pass out copies of page 17 to each person. Discuss each grouping so the children can see the range of sizes, shapes, and features that birds have. (You can also bring in the "props" listed in the materials section to help illustrate the discussion.) Here's some information you can use when you talk about each grouping.

The Largest Wingspans

Have the children point to the wandering albatross, the marabou stork, and the Andean condor. Explain that these three birds hold the three top records for the largest wingspans in the world. The wan-

Materials:
- copies of page 17
- drawing paper
- tiny jelly beans
- Ping-Pong balls
- yardsticks
- bird field guide
- tennis ball
- markers

Subject:
Science

dering albatross has the longest wings of any bird and is considered the most efficient flier of all. The stork and condor are also skilled fliers, but instead of having narrow, pointed wings, they have broad, slotted wings.

Have each person guess his or her own "armspan" and then have everyone pair up and measure each other's arms with a tape measure or yardstick. How does each compare to the top three birds?

The Tallest and the Heaviest

The largest bird living today is the ostrich. Males can grow to heights of over eight feet (2.4 m) and weigh over 345 pounds (155 kg). But the ostrich isn't the all-time record holder. The now-extinct moa of New Zealand was the tallest bird ever to live. It grew to heights of over 12 feet (3.6 m) and probably weighed over 500 pounds (225 kg). And the elephant bird of Madagascar, also extinct, was the heaviest bird ever to live. Some scientists think it weighed half a ton (454 kg)!

The Earliest Known Bird

Most scientists agree that birds evolved from reptiles millions of years ago. The earliest known bird was *Archaeopteryx*. It lived about 160 million years ago, during the Age of Dinosaurs. *Archaeopteryx* had many reptilelike features, such as bones in its tail, sharp teeth, and hooked claws. But it also had feathers, which is why it is considered a bird. Scientists think it was one of the first birds ever to have evolved.

Archaeopteryx

The Smallest Bird

The bee hummingbird of Cuba is the smallest bird in the world. It has a total length of two inches (5 cm), including its tail and its long bill. This tiny hummer weighs only about 1/10 ounce (2.8 g). That's about as much as a Ping-Pong ball.

The Fastest Fliers

The swift family includes some of the fastest fliers in the world. Some have been clocked at over 100 miles (160 km) per hour. Swifts spend most of their time on the wing, catching flying insects. In fact, they hold the record for spending the most time in the air.

Peregrine falcons are the fastest dive-bombing birds. When they swoop down on their prey, they can approach 200 miles (320 km) per hour.

The Largest Eyes

Birds have very large eyes in proportion to their bodies. In fact, some birds of prey and some running birds have bigger eyes than we do and can see a lot better. Ostriches have the biggest eyes of any land animal alive today. Each one is over two inches (5 cm) in diameter—about the size of a tennis ball. (Most of a bird's eye is hidden by the eyelids and the skull so it looks smaller than it really is.) Hawks and eagles probably have the sharpest vision of all animals.

The Largest and the Smallest Eggs

The ostrich holds the record for having the largest eggs of any living bird. Each one is about six inches (15 cm) long, with a very thick shell. (One ostrich egg is about 20 times bigger than a chicken egg.) But the elephant bird holds the record for having the largest bird eggs ever found. Each one could hold more than two gallons (7.6 l) and was over 10 inches (25 cm) long.

The tiniest eggs belong to the tiniest of birds—the hummingbirds. Their eggs are smaller than tiny jelly beans. (Pass around some small jelly beans.)

(continued next page)

Many birds can swim underwater using their wings as flippers. The fastest are penguins. Penguins are streamlined like missiles, and they can zip through the water at speeds of over 25 miles (40 km) per hour.

After discussing each category, ask the group what all these birds have in common. (All are warm-blooded and have feathers, beaks, wings, two legs, scales on their legs and feet, and many similar internal features, such as lightweight bones, fused bones, air sacs, and gizzards.)

After the discussion, take a trip to the zoo or take a bird walk in a nearby park. (The best time to go for a bird walk is very early in the morning when many birds are active.) Each time you see a bird, point out its special features, such as colors, wing shape, size, beak and feet adaptations, and songs. (If on a walk, use a field guide to help identify the birds you see.) Then have a contest. For example, of the birds you see, have your kids vote on the biggest bird, the smallest, the most colorful, the "weirdest," the one with the largest wingspan, the fastest hopper, the best glider, the loudest squawker, the one with the dullest colors, and the most common. Vote on each category and have the kids explain why they think something should "win" a certain title. Afterward, have them draw a picture of their favorite bird.

Flight of Fantasy

Listen to a story and imagine what it would be like to be a bird.

Objectives:
Describe the special characteristics that help a bird fly. Compare birds to people.

Ages:
Primary and Intermediate

Materials:
- *crayons*
- *pencils*
- *paper*
- *yardsticks*
- *tape*

Subjects:
Science, Creative Writing, and Art

hat would it be like to soar among the clouds or ride high on a thermal? In this activity your group will get a chance to imagine what it feels like to fly by listening to a very special story.

Have the kids close their eyes and take a few deep breaths. Tell them to relax their bodies and to let their imaginations soar as you read the following story out loud:

Flight of Fantasy

You are going to travel to places you've never been before, moving high above the earth. But first your body must change, for it is now too heavy and would never get off the ground.

Think of your feet and notice how they feel. Wiggle your toes and bend your ankles. Your feet begin to feel warm. Each ankle is getting squeezed and keeps growing until it is very skinny and long. One of your toes disappears and you now have only four. But not all face in the same direction. Three are held in front and one sticks out of the back of your foot. The end of each toe has a very sharp, curved toenail. You feel the outside of your feet and ankles slowly change from smooth skin to rough, bumpy scales. There is a perch in front of you and you hop over to it and feel your toes close around it. You are now perching.

Each leg becomes short and your knees pull up close to your body. You feel your body tip forward and become much shorter. All your insides shrink as your body becomes very slim and compact.

Suddenly heat fills your hands and arms. Your fingers almost dissolve and your hands grow very long and flat and wide. Now you have wings. Flap them a few times and feel how they move.

In a flash, your whole head feels warm and everything begins to change. Your teeth disappear and your nose and mouth grow together, getting very long and hard. Finally they form a sharp, curved beak—hooked and strong.

Your chin is gone now too, and each outer ear falls off. Now your eyes slide to the side of your head and they can no longer turn as easily in their sockets. You have to turn your whole head to look around. The ear holes move close to your eyes, beneath and behind them.

You're changing very quickly now! Each lung changes and air sacs appear in many places in your body. They are like thin balloons connected to your lungs. Air spaces invade your dense bones and make them much, much lighter than they were.

Hairs begin to grow all over your body. But wait, they're not hairs! They're feathers—covering you all over except for your beak and feet. Soft down feathers grow close to your body and longer, wider feathers cover your body, shape your wings and form a broad tail. When you try to speak, only a loud, hoarse call comes out.

A great urge to go outside comes over you and you hop down off your perch and hop quickly to the nearest door. As you face outside, the wind calls to you and you jump, flapping your wings quickly and with great force. Up you go—over the trees and buildings and toward the sky. A great, warm gust of wind pushes up under your wings and lifts you higher and higher until the trees look the size of buttons.

A mouse runs across a field far below you and you can see its shape very clearly, even though you are up so high. All of the colors of the earth look beautiful down below—green leaves, brown earth, and blue water. Buildings and cars of all colors are connected with roads that look like thin lines.

As you circle on the rising winds the breeze rushes around your body. You see a puffy, white cloud ahead, and with a few flaps of your wings and a tilt of your tail you glide into the whiteness. It is cool and damp and you feel lost for a moment. Then you come out on the other side and see a great range of mountains on the horizon.

The mountains and sky are your new home. As you fly high above the earth, you let out a long, loud cry. You are now called Eagle.

Have the children imagine that they are now back in their seats where they began their journey. Tell them to open their eyes slowly. Then have everyone stand up and stretch.

Ask them what their favorite part of the journey was. Discuss some of the changes that happened. Then have the children draw a picture of what they think the eagle might see as it looks down. How would trees look from above? Buildings? Water? Fields? You can also have them write a story that continues where the "Flight of Fantasy" left off.

Branching Out

Have the kids compare their "arm-spans" to the wingspan of an eagle. Divide the group into teams and give each team some masking tape and a yardstick. Have each team go to a different wall and measure out seven feet (2.1 m), the eagle's wingspan, marking the distance with two small pieces of tape. Then have each person go up to a wall and hold his or her arms out. How does each person's arm-span compare to an eagle's wingspan?

Prime Parts

Demonstrate how different parts of a bird's body work using a variety of everyday objects.

Objectives:
Describe how birds are adapted for flight. Compare bird adaptations to those of other animals.

Ages:
Primary and Intermediate

Materials (part 1):
- *chalkboard or easel paper*
- *elastic bands*
- *black construction paper*
- *soccer ball*

Materials (part 2):
- *different kinds of seeds*
- *small stones*
- *mortar and pestle*
- *a chicken gizzard (optional)*

Materials (part 3):
- *baby oil or petroleum jelly*
- *cotton cloth (about one square foot)*

Materials (part 4):
- *feathers (Get feathers only from a poultry farm or zoo; it's against the law to collect them.)*
- *overhead projector*
- *paper and pencils*
- *Velcro (20 inches)*
- *hand lens (optional)*

Materials (part 5):
- *chicken and beef bones (cleaned)*
- *strong light source (optional)*

Subject:
Science

Birds are unique. They have special body parts that set them apart from all other animals. In this demonstration/activity, your kids can learn about some of these special avian features as you discuss each one.

DEMONSTRATION #1: FOWL BALL

Ask the group if they think birds have good vision. Then draw an outline of a bird's head on the board or on a large piece of easel paper. Ask if a bird's eyes are located more on the sides of the head or on the front of the head. (In most birds, the eyes are on the side. But in some owls and hawks, the eyes face forward.) Then have someone come up and draw in the bird's eyes.

Next have each person look at his or her neighbor to see where human eyes are located. (They face forward.) Explain that people have *binocular vision*, which means both eyes focus on the same image. Most birds have *monocular vision* most of the time because each eye focuses on a different image. Most birds have binocular vision only when they focus straight ahead with both eyes focused on the same image.

Then have each person gently shut one eye or cover one eye with a hand and look around. Ask if they can tell a difference between one-eyed sight and two-eyed sight. (Animals with binocular vision can judge

distance better than those with monocular vision.)

To demonstrate the difference, have everyone make an eye patch using a piece of black construction paper stapled to an elastic band. Take the group outside and have everyone put on his or her eye patch. Then make a large circle and play catch. Is it any harder to catch a ball when seeing out of only one eye?

DEMONSTRATION #2: GIZZARD GRINDERS

Birds do not have teeth, but they do have a grinding muscular stomach called the *gizzard*. Many birds also swallow grit (small pebbles, stones, eggshells, and other hard materials), which ends up in the gizzard and helps grind seeds, bones, and other hard-to-digest food.

To show your group how the gizzard grinds, bring in some cracked corn, sunflower seeds, or other nuts or seeds, and grind them up using a few stones in a mortar and pestle. Pass around the powder and explain that the churning motion you

used is similar to the muscular action in the gizzard of a seed-eating bird—except that a bird's gizzard is much stronger. (One study showed that a turkey could grind up 24 English walnuts, shell and all, in just four hours. Another study showed that a turkey could even grind steel needles to pieces.)

Tell your group that the gizzard helps birds get the most nutrients from the food they eat. That means they can get more energy from less food, which saves them time looking for food.

Note: You might also want to pass around a real chicken or turkey gizzard (you can get one in a whole chicken or turkey at the supermarket) so the kids can feel how thick and tough the gizzard muscles are. Cut it open to show the tough inner lining.

DEMONSTRATION #3: A HANDY GLAND

Another "part" that birds have that other animals don't have is an oil gland. The oil gland, or preen gland, is on the bird's rump, right above the base of the tail. The gland secretes an oil that the bird squeezes out with its bill and spreads on its feathers and feet. The oil helps keep the feathers waterproof, flexible, and in good condition.

To show your group how the oil helps waterproof the feathers so water doesn't soak in and weight the bird down, try this demonstration. Cut two 6 x 12" (15 x 30-cm) pieces of cotton cloth. Apply petroleum jelly or baby oil to one of the pieces. Dip each into a cup of water and then pull them both out. The water soaks into the cloth without oil but runs off the other.

DEMONSTRATION #4: FEATHER FEATURES

Birds are the only animals in the world with feathers. In this demonstration, your kids can learn the parts of a feather and how feathers help a bird fly and stay warm.

Explain that there are two main types of feathers: *contour feathers*, which are found on the bird's body, wings, and tail; and *down feathers*, which are fluffier and softer and lie close to a bird's body, under the contour feathers.

Then explain that the vane is made up of hundreds of *barbs* that look like skinny hairs coming off the shaft in parallel rows. To show the barbs, place a large contour feather on an overhead projector. The enlarged silhouette will show how the barbs stick out from the shaft. It will also show the tiny *barbules* that grow off from each of the barbs. Explain that the barbules have rolled edges on one side and tiny hooks on the other that interlock side by side and hold the barbs together—kind of like a "ziplock" seal. This "ziplock" system is one of the most important flight features a bird has. The flat, flexible vane stays locked in flight, helping the bird keep its smooth, streamlined shape and allowing each feather to firmly fan the air. But if the vane does split apart between two barbs, the bird can "zip" its feathers back into shape by pressing the barbs together with its beak. This is one reason birds *preen*—it helps them fix their feathers and get them back into shape for flying. (See page 41 for more about preening.)

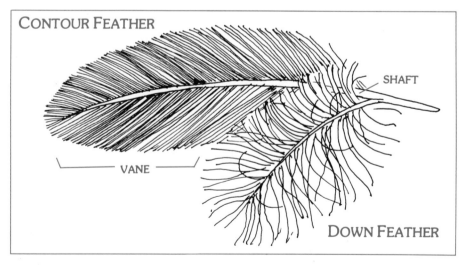

CONTOUR FEATHER

SHAFT

VANE

DOWN FEATHER

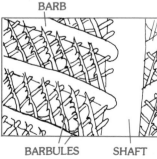

BARB

BARBULES   SHAFT

If possible, give each person a contour feather and a down feather. (You can get feathers at a poultry farm or zoo.) Tell each person to look closely at the contour feather. Explain that the hard center tube is called the *shaft* and the rest of the feather is called the *vane*. Have each person draw a picture of his or her feather and label the vane and the shaft (see diagram).

Another way to demonstrate the hooking system is to pass out a tiny piece of Velcro to each person. Have everyone seal the Velcro and pull it apart. Then have everyone look at the two parts of the Velcro under a hand lens or magnifying glass. Each person should be able to see the tiny hooks and loops. (This is not exactly the same as a bird's feather, but it's close.) *(continued next page)*

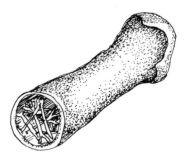

DEMONSTRATION #5: BONING UP ON BIRDS

Bird bones are not only lightweight but also very strong. That's because they are hollow or partially hollow, and some have thin reinforcing braces inside for support. To compare bird bones with those of other animals, bring in several chicken bones as well as bones from a cow, lamb, or other mammal. (You can get bones from the butcher or nature center, or you can save some from a meal.)

Let the children examine the bones to see how they are different. If possible, saw through a chicken wing bone. Show the children the very thin crisscross pattern inside. (Warn them to be careful of sharp edges.) You can also hold a chicken bone and a cow bone up to a strong light to show the difference between bird and mammal bones. You can see light through the chicken bone but not through the denser cow bone.

Pass the Part

Play a soda straw relay game.

Objective:
Describe four characteristics that make a bird a bird.

Ages:
Intermediate and Advanced

Materials:
- *blank white paper*
- *markers*
- *plastic straws for each person*
- *large sheets of easel paper*
- *tape or thumbtacks*
- *copies of the clues on page 15 (one for each team)*
- *scissors*
- *quarters*
- *chalkboard (optional)*

Subject:
Science

I n this game, your group can review bird characteristics by playing a team relay race called "Pass the Part." Before you start, read the group this poem as an introduction:

A Lizard Has No Gizzard

A lizard has no gizzard,
And a camel has no bill.
And you'll never see a shark soar
Like a turkey vulture will.

Bear bones don't have struts inside,
And wallabies don't have wings.
And you'll never see a kangaroo
That twitters, squawks, or sings.

A cheetah doesn't ever
Have a feather or a crop.
And a giraffe can't fly 500 miles
Without a single stop.

An octopus has no air sacs,
A squid never did have down,
And you'll rarely see an earthworm
That's any color but dull brown.

But birds have feathers, wings, and crops,
And a gizzard and a beak.
With dazzling colors and awesome flight,
They really are unique!

After reading the poem, talk about the characteristics that make a bird so different from other animals. (See the background information on pages 4-6.) For older kids,

compare birds to other animal groups, such as fish, mammals, reptiles, amphibians, and insects. For example, birds have a gizzard to grind their food, but many other animals have teeth. Birds can see color, but many mammals, such as dogs, cannot. After your discussion, play this relay game about bird parts:

SETTING UP

1. Divide your group into teams of four or five. Give each team a large piece of paper, a quarter, several sheets of blank paper, several pairs of scissors, and markers.
2. Draw this bird picture on a chalkboard or large piece of easel paper so all the teams can see it. Then have one person in each team copy the picture onto the large piece of paper. Another person on the team can draw in the circles by tracing around the quarters. (Make sure the circles are numbered as they are on the model.)
3. Each team will also need to cut out eight circles from the blank paper. (Again, have them trace around the quarters.) Then have them label each circle as follows: gizzard, air sacs, oil gland, feather, wing, crop, ears, and bones.
4. Now clear the room and form relay lines, with the kids in each team lining up one behind the other. Place a desk or table in front of each team and lay out the eight circles on the desk. Then put a copy of

the clues (below) next to each set of circles. (Don't copy the answers shown in parentheses.)

5. On the wall (or on a bulletin board)

6. Give each person a plastic straw.

behind each team, hang the team's large bird picture. Roll a piece of tape and stick it in the center of each circle.

HOW TO PLAY

The first person in each team is the leader. The leader must read Clue #1 on the clue sheet and decide which circle fits the clue best. Then the leader must pick up the circle with his or her straw by placing the end of the straw against the circle and sucking in. The leader must pass the circle to the next person in line without letting it fall off the end of the straw. The next person then must pass it to the third person in line. Have the kids keep passing the circle from straw to straw until it's

sucked up by the last person. Then the last person can carry the circle to the big bird and tape it onto the right number. (Clue #1 goes in circle #1.) The last person should then hurry to the front of the line, read Clue #2, pick up the appropriate circle, and pass it down the line. Again, the last person must tape the circle onto the bird in the correctly numbered circle; then he or she becomes the leader for round three. As soon as one team finishes its bird, the game is over.

HOW TO SCORE

The team that finishes first gets ten points. But each team also gets five points for every circle that is in the correct spot. If the fastest team has all the circles filled in

correctly, it wins. But if it missed some, another team can still win. As you score, discuss each clue so that everyone understands the answers.

RULES AND REMINDERS

- No one is allowed to use his or her hands as the circle is being passed along. (Only after the last person has sucked up the circle can he or she touch it.)
- If the circle should drop before it gets to the end of the line, it must be placed back on the desk or table, and the team must start that round again. (If your kids keep

dropping the circles, don't make them start at the beginning. Just let them suck the circles off the ground and keep passing them along.)

- Teams should be far enough apart so that they cannot see which circles are being picked up by other team leaders.

PASS THE PART CLUES

1. I'm strong and thick and can really do the trick,
   Especially with a lot of grit.
   (gizzard)
2. Millions of barbs on every vane,
   Without me winter would be a pain.
   (feather)
3. My shape gives birds something really neat:
   A lift to get them off their feet. (wing)
4. Space inside to keep me light,
   Struts that brace to give me might.
   (bone)
5. I'm not a friend of water—
   that's a fact!

And I'm a big part of the preening act.
(oil gland)
6. Two small holes are the only clues
   That we're inside a bird, hidden from view.
   (ears)
7. Depending on what a bird might eat,
   I can double my size—
   that's quite a feat!
   (crop)
8. In some birds we're found almost everywhere.
   We're hooked to the lungs and fill up with air.
   (air sacs)

The Largest Wingspans

Wandering Albatross (almost a 12-foot wingspan)

Marabou Stork (10-foot wingspan)

Andean Condor (10-foot wingspan)

The Fastest Fliers

Swifts (fly at speeds of over 100 miles per hour)

The Fastest Swimmers

Penguins (can swim over 25 miles per hour)

The Largest Eyes
Ostriches and Birds of Prey

The Earliest Known Bird
Archaeopteryx (lived 160 million years ago during the Age of Dinosaurs)

The Largest Egg
Ostrich Egg (6 inches long)

The Smallest Egg
Hummingbird Egg

The Smallest Bird
Bee Hummingbird (2 inches long)

The Tallest Bird Ever to Live
Moa (over 12 feet tall)

The Tallest Bird Alive Today
Ostrich (over 8 feet tall and weighs over 345 pounds)

The Heaviest Bird Ever to Live

Elephant Bird (weighed half a ton)

FAMILY LIFE

t was 5:00 AM on a Saturday morning in early spring and George was wide awake. Outside he could hear loud tweets, twitters, warbles, chirps, and cries. "Every bird within 50 miles must be singing its heart out in my yard!" George mumbled, pulling his window shut with a bang. Crawling back into bed, he wondered what in the world all those birds could be so happy about.

The Season for Singing

George didn't realize it, but the birds outside his window weren't singing for joy. To a bird, singing is serious business—an important part of the breeding season. That's because singing is a bird's way of staking out a breeding territory, defending the territory, and—at least for some species—attracting a mate. (Mockingbirds, Carolina wrens, and a few other birds sometimes sing later in the year, when they're setting up and defending winter territories. But singing is usually much more common and energetic in the springtime.)

Male songbirds usually do all of the singing, although female cardinals, grosbeaks, and a few other females sometimes sing too. A bird's song means different things to different birds in the "neighborhood." To the males, it usually means "Keep off, this is my place!" But to females of the same species it may say,"Here I am and I'm looking for a mate!"

How do birds "become" singers? Through research, ornithologists (scientists who study birds) have discovered that some birds *learn* the characteristic song of their species by hearing other birds sing it. But the songs of some other birds are completely *innate*. That means that a bird "knows" and can sing its species' song without ever having to hear it. For many birds, song is somewhere in-between—partially learned and partially innate. (See "How Do They Know," *Ranger Rick,* Jan 83, pages 28-31, for more information about learned and innate behavior.)

Songs vs. Calls: A bird's song is usually made up of several notes that the bird sings in a regular pattern, over and over again. Sometimes a singer will vary its song slightly, but the overall pattern of notes stays the same.

Not *every* note a bird utters is part of its song, though. Birds also have *calls*—sounds they make during feeding, migration, or when danger is near. Unlike songs, calls are usually short—made up of only one or a few short notes.

Thump, Strut, and Bow: Not all birds are singers. But some of the ones that aren't make different kinds of noises to defend their territories or attract mates. For example, male ruffed grouse make low thumping sounds by standing on logs and beating the air with their wings. Some male woodpeckers can make a lot of noise by hammering away on hollow tree branches and sometimes even metal gutters and other objects. And male prairie chickens strut, bow, and make strange whistling sounds by blowing up air sacs on their necks.

Displays That Dazzle: Singing, hammering, and thumping all help different kinds of birds find each other during the breeding season. But for many birds, sight is much more important than sound when it comes to finding a mate. Color, special courtship feathers, and movements all play a big part in some birds' courtship displays. Male peacocks, for example, parade in front of the females, fanning and shaking some of their long, colorful feathers. Male frigatebirds court females by filling up their bright red throat sacs with air. And some male birds of paradise hang upside down to show off their bright feathers.

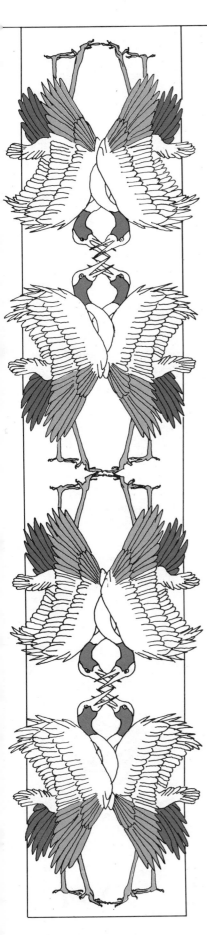

All Kinds of Nests

Once a bird has found a mate, nest-building can get underway. Sometimes, depending on the species, the male and female work together; at other times just one of the two will build the nest.

When most of us think of a bird's nest, we think of the typical twig, grass, and mud "cup" that a lot of songbirds build. But birds' nests come in a lot of different shapes and sizes. Some birds—many owls and hawks, for example—don't build nests at all, but use old crow, heron, or other nests instead. Many seabirds lay their eggs on bare rock, and a lot of other birds just scrape out small depressions in bare sand or soil. Other ground-nesting birds, such as most ducks and geese, build nests of reeds, grasses, weeds, or sticks.

Keeping the Eggs Warm

All birds lay eggs, and most birds *incubate* their eggs, or keep them warm, with the heat of their own bodies. (A few birds bury their eggs in dark sand, in warm soil next to hot springs, or in fermenting vegetation—all of which produce enough heat to hatch the eggs.)

In several bird species the male and female take turns keeping the *clutch*, or group of eggs in the nest, warm. And there are a few species in which both parents sit on the clutch at the same time. But when one parent is more colorful than the other, the drabber, harder-to-see parent usually does most of the incubating. That's why female cardinals, goldfinches, and most other female songbirds usually spend more time on the nest than their colorful mates do.

Hatching Out

After as few as 11 days or as many as 90 days, depending on the species, a young bird is ready to hatch out of its egg. Using the sharp "egg-tooth" on the top of its beak, the young bird slowly chips away at its eggshell, usually without any help from its parents. Several hours (or sometimes even days) later, it breaks free of the egg.

Some newly-hatched birds are blind, naked, and unable to care for themselves. These helpless, or *altricial*, birds stay in the nest until they *fledge*, or take their first flights. They're fed by their parents, who make trip after trip to the nest with insects and other high-protein food. (Even after they fledge, many altricial birds continue to be fed by their parents for awhile.) Most songbirds, owls, woodpeckers, and parrots are altricial.

Turkeys, grouse, ducks, geese, and many other ground-nesting birds are *precocial*. Unlike altricial birds, precocial chicks can see well and are covered with down feathers when they hatch. In almost no time at all they can run around and even find their own food.

Some birds aren't completely altricial or precocial, but are somewhere in-between.

Bird Talk

Sing a bird song, imitate bird sounds, and make up bird songs and calls.

Objectives:
Describe the songs and calls of a few common birds. Give one reason why birds sing and call.

Ages:
Primary

Materials:
- *pictures of birds (optional)*
- *bird records (optional)*

Subject:
Science

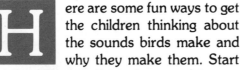

Here are some fun ways to get the children thinking about the sounds birds make and why they make them. Start by asking the kids if they have any ideas as to why birds sing. Explain that birds have several ways of communicating with each other and discuss the uses of bird songs and calls in attracting mates, staking out and defending territories, and in giving warnings. (See pages 18 and 42.)

After talking about bird songs and calls, try some of these activities:

Singing With the Birds—Young kids can learn some of the calls of a few common birds by singing the following verses to the tune of "Old MacDonald." Show the children pictures of each type of bird as they sing about it. Afterward, talk about the different birds and make up new verses of your own.

1. Black-cap is a chickadee
   e-i-e-i-o
   She's as tiny as can be
   e-i-e-i-o
   With a *dee-dee* here and a *dee-dee* there
   Here a *dee*, there a *dee*, everywhere a *dee-dee*
   Black-cap is a chickadee
   e-i-e-i-o
2. Bobwhite is a little quail
   e-i-e-i-o
   Round and plump and short of tail
   e-i-e-i-o
   With a *bobwhite* here and a *bobwhite* there
   Here a *bob*, there a *white*, everywhere a *bobwhite* . . . etc.
3. Stella is a Steller's Jay
   e-i-e-i-o
   She always has too much to say
   e-i-e-i-o
   With a *squawk-squawk* here and a *squawk-squawk* there . . . etc.
4. Hunter is a great horned owl
   e-i-e-i-o
   Night is when he's on the prowl
   e-i-e-i-o
   With a *hoot-hoot* here and a *hoot-hoot* there . . . etc.

Musical Names—Explain to the children that some birds are named for the sounds of their calls. The chickadee, bobwhite, whip-poor-will, and killdeer are all examples of birds that "say" their name. If possible, play a few recordings of some of these calls. (You may be able to check out bird records from your local library.) Then have the kids make up calls for their own names and perform them for the rest of the group.

Calling All Birds—Most of the noises birds make come from voice boxes in the lower part of their windpipes. People's voice boxes are in the upper part of their windpipes and produce sound in a different way. But it can be fun to try to imitate the songs or calls of birds. Try holding a contest to see who is the best bird imitator in your group. Play a call from a bird album and have four or five kids try to imitate it. The rest of the group can vote on who they think did the best job. Then pick another bird song or call, four or five new kids, and repeat the contest. Make sure you give everyone a chance to imitate a bird. The winner of each bird call can compete against the other winners for the title of "Best Bird Imitator."

Make-Believe Birds—Divide the children into groups of two or three and let them make up a song and/or calls for an imaginary bird. They should make up a song, a warning call, and any others they want to add. Then have each group demonstrate their calls and/or songs to the rest of the kids.

Leonard Lee Rue III great horned owl

A Bird Family Album

Draw bird pictures and create a bird family album.

Objective:
Describe the family life of one bird.

Ages:
Primary and Intermediate

Materials:
- *bird and nest field guides and bird reference books*
- *drawing paper*
- *construction paper*
- *pencils and crayons*
- *stapler*

Subjects:
Science, Art, and Creative Writing

Your kids can learn about the family lives of different birds by making their own bird family albums. Here's how:

Explain that everyone will be creating a bird "photo album" that traces the family life of a particular bird. Then let each child choose a bird to work with. Next have each person fold several pieces of construction paper in half, stack the pieces along the folded edge, and staple the pieces together. Then have the kids draw pictures that will go into their albums. For example, they could draw a picture of their particular bird's egg, nest, and parents. (Have them use field guides and reference books while they're drawing.) Then they can glue the finished pictures into their albums and label them.

Here are some sample labels you might want to suggest to the kids to give them some ideas for pictures: My Parents, My Egg, Me—Just After Hatching, My Brothers and Sisters and I in the Nest, Our Family Portrait, Getting My First Meal, At the Wintering Grounds, My Mate and I Building Our First Nest.

When the kids finish, have them share their albums with the rest of the group. Talk about some of the differences among the kinds of birds they chose.

American kestrels

cattle egrets

Leonard Lee Rue III great horned owls

glaucous-winged gulls

BRANCHING OUT: CREATIVE WRITING

Have the kids write a paragraph about the birds they've chosen using 15 of the following 20 words: altricial, brood, cavity, clutch, courtship, cowbird, defend, egg, fledge, hatch, incubate, migrate, molt, nest, parasite, precocial, predator, sing, territory, young.

Objectives:
*Describe the nests of
three common birds.
Build a specific type of
bird nest, using the same
materials a bird would
use.*

Ages:
*Primary and
Intermediate*

Materials:
- *copies of page 25*
- *bird research books*
- *slips of paper*
- *pencils*
- *nesting materials*

Subject:
Science

Birds build their nests in all kinds of places. Some nest high in trees while others nest on the ground. Some plaster their nests on the sides of buildings or rocky cliffs and others build floating nests in marshy areas. Many birds also nest in tree cavities, stream banks, fields, and swamps. Birds also use a variety of nesting materials to build their nests, including sticks, mud, stones, lichens, grass, spider webs, snakeskins, and thistledown.

Some birds are adaptable nest builders. It seems they'll build their nests wherever they can find a spot and use whatever materials they can find. But other birds are much pickier and will build their nests only in certain places and use only certain materials.

In this activity, your kids can pick the perfect site to build a nest and then try to build one themselves. (Although most primary-age children can't do the research part of this activity, they can go on a hike to look for nests and good nesting sites, and try to build their own nests.) First write

Luise Woelflein

down on slips of paper the names of five common birds that live in your area. (Choose birds that nest in your schoolyard or in a nearby park.) Divide the group into five teams and have each team pick one slip. Then explain that each team is a real estate agent hired by the bird on their slip of paper to find the perfect nest site.

Pass out copies of page 25 to each person. Explain that each person in the team must research their bird to fill out the nesting information sheet. (You can have them work in teams too.)

After everyone has filled out the information, take the group to a nearby park (or schoolyard or nature center) that has several different types of habitats. Have the kids in each team search for the perfect spot to build a nest. Remind them that most birds build their nests near a food source and that the nests are usually sheltered from rain, hot sun, and other types of weather. Also tell them that many birds hide their nests so predators can't spot them.

Give everyone 15 minutes to find the perfect spot and then have everyone gather back together. Start with one team and have the kids in the team describe their bird and its requirements for a home. Then visit the nest site and talk about the pros and cons of the location. (This one's too exposed, this one's too far from water, this one would get run over by a lawnmower, and so on.) After visiting all the nest sites for one type of bird, take a vote on which team found the best site.

Afterward, have each group work together to try to build the nest of their bird, using the same materials the bird would use. Each nest should also be the correct size and shape. Have everyone on the team pitch in to help gather the materials and shape the nest. (Warn the children not to pick flowers or pull living plants.) Then line up the nests and talk about each one. Encourage the children to look out for nests when they take walks with their parents or friends. But remind them that it's against the law to remove or damage a nest in the wild, even if it is old and abandoned.

The Incredible Egg

Put together a model bird egg and talk about an egg's different parts.

Objective:
Describe the structure of a fertilized bird egg.

Ages:
Primary, Intermediate, and Advanced

Materials:
- *plastic pantyhose eggs (1 per person)*
- *plastic bags (2 per egg)*
- *balloons (2 per egg)*
- *white tissue paper*
- *masking tape*
- *modeling clay*
- *toothpicks*
- *glue*
- *tempera paints or crayons*
- *black markers*

Subjects:
Science and Art

Bird eggs are protective life-support systems complete with all the nutrients, minerals, and water a developing bird needs before it hatches. In this activity your kids can take a close-up look at eggs by making their own egg models. But before the kids start on their egg models, make one yourself to use in a discussion about eggs. (See the instructions on page 24.) Here's a look at the main parts of an egg containing a growing embryo:

- **Amnion**—The amnion is a sac full of liquid that envelops the developing bird and protects its delicate tissues.
- **Yolk Sac**—The yolk sac contains the developing bird's food source, the yolk. The yolk is made up of proteins, fats, and carbohydrates and is connected to the bird by blood vessels that spread out across the sac's surface. A day or two before hatching, what's left of the yolk sac and yolk is drawn into the bird's abdomen through its umbilical cord. For a while after it hatches, the bird can use this leftover yolk as an extra food source.
- **Allantois**—The allantois is the developing bird's saclike breathing organ and the storage place for its waste products.
- **Chorion**—The chorion is a membrane that envelops the allantois, yolk sac, and the amnion.

- **Albumen**—This is the egg white. It is mostly water with about 10% protein and a small amount of minerals. The albumen keeps the embryo from drying out, helps support the yolk, and is a source of protein and minerals for the embryonic bird. Most of it will be used by the embryo during its development.
- **Shell Membranes**—There is an inner and an outer shell membrane. The two membranes are fused together and to the shell except at the wide end of the egg. Here the inner shell membrane separates from the outer shell membrane, forming a pocket of air. Before breaking, or *pipping,* the shell, the fully developed bird will break through the inner shell membrane to this pocket and breathe air for the first time.
- **Shell**—The shell protects the egg and keeps it from drying out. It's mostly made up of calcium carbonate, some of which will be broken down and used to develop the bones of the embryo. (This breakdown of calcium carbonate also weakens the shell, making it easier for the young bird to hatch.)

Though the shell appears completely solid, its surface is permeated by thousands of microscopic holes, or *pores.* The embryo exchanges oxygen and carbon dioxide through these pores.

(continued next page)

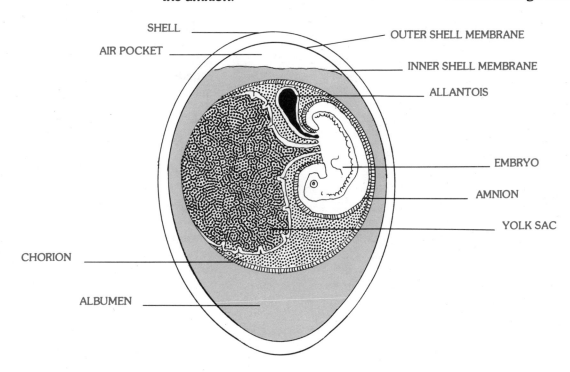

SHELL

AIR POCKET

OUTER SHELL MEMBRANE

INNER SHELL MEMBRANE

ALLANTOIS

EMBRYO

AMNION

YOLK SAC

CHORION

ALBUMEN

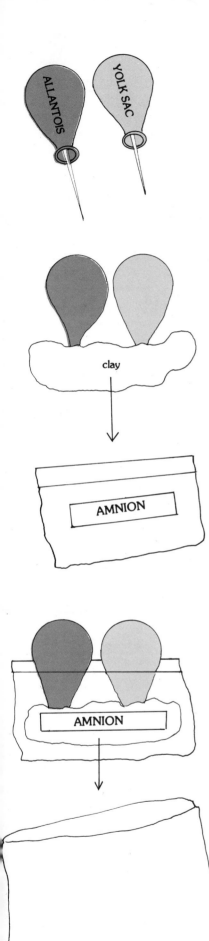

THE MAKING OF AN EGG

You can think of the different parts of an egg as being layers that are added one at a time from the inside out. As a yolk passes through the *oviduct,* or egg-laying tube, each layer—the albumen, inner and outer shell membranes, and finally the shell—is added in turn. And just a few hours before being laid, the egg receives its pigmentation. The pigments are produced in the bird's body. And because each egg is colored separately, there is a lot of variation even in eggs laid by the same bird. Each species, though, generally lays eggs of a similar color and shape.

Female birds can lay eggs that haven't been fertilized. But these unfertilized eggs will never develop an amnion, allantois, chorion, or embryo. The chicken eggs you buy in the grocery store are unfertilized eggs.

THE INCREDIBLE EGG MODEL

Here's how to make one:
1. Color the insides of both halves of a large plastic egg with tempera paint or a crayon. This represents the outer shell membrane.
2. Glue a piece of tissue paper to the inside of each half of the shell to represent the inner shell membrane. In the wider half of the shell the tissue paper should be glued so that there is an air space between it and the "bottom" of the shell. (This space is the air pocket.) Trim off any excess paper from the edges of the shell and make sure the halves still fit together.
3. Shape some modeling clay into an "embryonic bird." (Any shape will do.)
4. Use two small, differently colored balloons for the allantois and the yolk sac. Label them both with a marker, then glue a toothpick into each one so that most of the toothpick sticks out from the neck of the balloon (see picture).
5. Write "amnion" on a piece of masking tape and stick the tape onto one of the plastic bags. Then write "chorion" on a second piece of masking tape and stick it onto the second plastic bag.

You are now ready to assemble your egg. Here's how:
1. Stick the balloons into one side of the modeling clay, using the toothpicks. The embryo now has its allantois and yolk sac.
2. Place the embryo within the bag labeled "amnion" so that the bag covers the embryo and just the necks of the balloons. Lightly press the plastic against the clay so that it does not slip.
3. Place the amnion, embryo, allantois, and yolk sac within the bag labeled "chorion."
4. Place everything into the bigger half of the shell and close.
5. Use a crayon to draw dots (pores) on the outside of the shell.

The kids can take their eggs apart and put them back together as many times as they like. You might want to have them repeat the names and functions of the different parts as they do this.

BRANCHING OUT: ART

Have the kids use crayons, tempera paints, and other art supplies to color the outsides of their eggs the way different birds' eggs are colored. You might want to provide pictures of different eggs. (See *A Field Guide to Birds' Nests* and *A Field Guide to Western Birds' Nests* in the Peterson Field Guide Series or *The Birds* by Roger Tory Peterson and The Editors of Life.)

Have each child pick a particular egg to color. Or have the kids create their own camouflaged eggs and then have them explain how their eggs' colors protect the developing birds.

1. Name of your bird. _____

2. Draw a picture of your bird on the back of this sheet.

3. Describe your bird's habitat. _____

_____

_____

_____

4. What does your bird eat? _____

_____

_____

_____

5. What kind of nest does it build or use? _____

_____

_____

6. Draw a picture of the nest.

7. Where does your bird usually nest? _____

_____

8. What time of year does your bird nest? _____

9. How many eggs does it lay? _____

10. Draw a picture of the eggs.

FINDING A PLACE TO LIVE

n a steamy rain forest in South America, a flock of colorful parrots swoops down to feed on the ripe fruits of a tropical tree. In Antarctica, thousands of penguins plunge into the icy waters to gorge on tiny shrimplike krill. And high in the Himalayan Mountains a huge bearded vulture carefully scans the valleys, hoping to spot a meal of rotting meat. From fruit to krill to dead animals, you'll find birds eating all kinds of foods. And you'll find birds living almost everywhere.

Habitat Is Home: A bird's home is called its *habitat.* And birds, like all animals, live in habitats that provide them with *food, water, shelter,* and *space* to mate, raise their young, and grow. (Some migrating birds breed in one area and winter in another. Both habitats supply food, water, and shelter; but only one is used for raising young.) Some birds have very specific habitat needs and can live only in certain areas. Others are very adaptable and can live in many different types of habitats.

Amazing Adaptations: Take a look at the birds in your backyard. You'll see all kinds of different beaks, feet, body shapes and sizes, colors, and behaviors. Why are birds that live in the same basic habitat so different? If all birds looked the same, ate the same foods, lived in exactly the same place, and had the same habits, they would all be competing for the same food, water, shelter, and space. So instead, birds, like all other animals, fill different *niches* or "jobs" in the habitats where they live. For example, if you watch the birds in your backyard, you'll see that some are gobbling insects or fruits, others are crunching seeds, and a few may be capturing small mammals. Some feed at night, others feed in the day. Some use mud to build their nests, others use sticks. And some nest in holes while others nest on the ground.

Adapting, Hawaiian Style: Adapting to fill a niche doesn't happen overnight—it takes many, many generations for the changes to occur. And adaptations can happen along with a big change in the environment, such as a volcanic eruption, an ice age, or a major earthquake. Adaptations can also occur when new species arrive on an island or spread out to a remote area.

For example, honeycreepers are small songbirds that live in Hawaii. When the ancestors of the honeycreepers first flew to Hawaii, millions of years ago, there weren't many other birds on the islands. The newly arrived birds eventually spread to many different types of habitats. (Many ornithologists think that these birds were seed eaters that had flown across the Pacific from the east Asian mainland, although no one really knows for sure.) Because there wasn't competition from other birds, the honeycreepers slowly began to fill different niches. For example, one day, just by chance, a honeycreeper chick hatched that was different from the other chicks. It had a slightly stronger beak than all the others. It could eat many of the hard-coated seeds that grew on Hawaii that the other honeycreepers couldn't break apart. Eventually, this strong-beaked bird mated and had chicks. And some of its chicks also had a stronger-type beak. After many many generations, more and more strong-beaked honeycreepers survived, and eventually two different kinds (species) of honeycreepers were on the island—those with regular beaks and those with beaks that could crack especially hard seeds.

Other traits also became common among the honeycreepers—long, curved beaks for probing flowers; sharp, tweezerlike beaks for catching insects; and stout, curved beaks for grabbing fruit. In fact, scientists think that there were over 39 different species of honeycreepers on the Hawaiian Islands, each with slightly

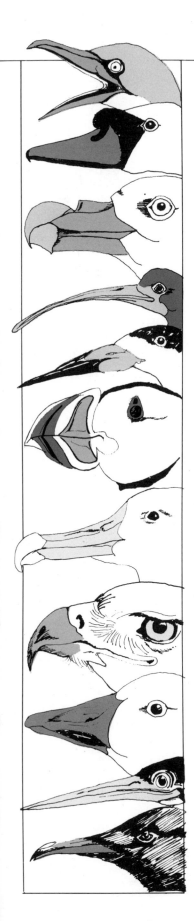

different habits and food preferences. (Today, due to habitat loss and other factors, only eight species remain.)

Most changes that happen in a population don't get passed along, though. For example, what if one of the honeycreepers had been born with a weaker heart or long wings that made it hard to fly in the strong island winds? These traits would not have helped it survive, and it probably would have died before it mated. Usually, only those special characteristics that help a bird survive or ones that don't hinder its survival get passed along. And even then it takes many, many generations for the trait to become common.

A Beakful of Birds: One of the best ways to see how birds adapt to their habitats is to take a close-up look at their beaks. Bird beaks come in all shapes and sizes and each is specially suited for finding and eating the type of food its owner needs.

Some Neat Feet: Birds' feet, and especially their toes, come in a variety of shapes and sizes—just as their beaks do. And each foot is well suited to how a bird lives. Most birds have four toes on each foot and all birds have a claw at the tip of each toe. But different birds have different-sized toes and claws and a different arrangement of the toes, with some facing forward and others facing backward. (What most people think of as a bird's feet are really just its toes. The actual foot extends to the backward bend in its leg. The bend is the bird's ankle, not its knee.)

Bye-Bye, Birdies: Many birds have a summer home and winter home, and each year they make the same round trip flight, or *migration,* from one home to the other. Birds usually migrate to a new habitat to escape changing seasons. In North America, many insect-eating, fruit-eating, and nectar-sipping birds can't find enough food to keep them alive during the cold snowy winters in the northern part of Canada and the United States. So these birds migrate south to warmer climates where food is plentiful. In the tropics, many birds migrate during the dry season, when food sources die and water sources dry up.

How Do They Know Where They're Going? One of the most amazing things about migration is that birds end up in the same places every year. And for some birds, that means navigating in the right direction for over 10,000 miles (16,000 km).

Many scientists think that different types of birds use different cues to help them navigate. Daytime migrants seem to use the sun to point them in the right direction, while many nighttime fliers use the stars as their guide. Other birds rely on landmarks such as mountains, lakes, and rivers to let them know where they are. And some birds seem to use the earth's magnetic pull, and even their hearing, to steer them in the right direction. Scientists think many birds also use a combination of these navigational "tricks" to help them find their way.

How Do They Know When to Go? Most birds that migrate are born with the "drive" to migrate. Their bodies are programmed, like a computer, telling them where to go, when to stop, and how to get back. But even though the urge to migrate is instinctive, many scientists think that shorter daylight hours in late summer trigger chemical changes in their bodies that help them physically get ready for the long journey. These chemical changes sometimes trigger molting, as well as the "push" to gain an extra layer of fat.

Feet Are Neat

Match birds to their feet and mold bird feet out of clay.

Objective:
Describe several types of bird feet and explain how each helps a bird survive in its habitat.

Ages:
Primary and Intermediate

Materials:
- *copies of page 39*
- *clay or modeling dough*
- *pipe cleaners*
- *tape*
- *markers, crayons, or colored pencils*
- *white cardboard or stiff white paper*

Subjects:
Science and Art

One good way for kids to understand how birds are adapted to live in their habitats is for them to take a look at bird feet. Since different types of birds use their feet in different ways, bird feet come in a lot of different shapes and sizes.

Ask your group to think of some of the ways birds use their feet. (They use them for walking, perching, swimming, running, climbing, and grabbing.) Then talk about some of the different kinds of feet different birds have. Here are some examples:

- Climbers—Woodpeckers have two toes in front and two toes in back for climbing up and down tree trunks.
- Graspers—Hawks, owls, and other birds of prey have large curved claws, called *talons,* that dig into their prey and help them hold onto it in flight.
- Perchers—Robins, mourning doves, and many other birds have three toes that face forward and one long hind toe that helps them grip their perches tightly.

- Runners—Ostriches and killdeer have two and three toes, respectively (instead of four), and all their toes point forward for fast running.
- Scratchers—Pheasants, chickens, and other chickenlike birds have rakelike toes for scratching in the soil.
- Swimmers—Ducks, coots, and other swimmers use their feet as paddles.

Next pass out copies of page 39 to the group and have them try to figure out which birds go with which feet. Then pass out lumps of clay or modeling dough and have everyone make a model of bird feet. (They can each pick one of the birds on the Copycat Page or they can pick different birds.) When they're finished, have each person draw a picture of his or her bird on a piece of white cardboard or stiff white paper, color it, and tape pipe cleaner legs to the cardboard. (To make each leg, have them twist two pipe cleaners together.) Then they can push the legs, with the bodies attached, down into the feet.

BRANCHING OUT: TAKE A HIKE

Take your group on a bird walk to look at different kinds of bird feet. Each time you spot a bird, talk about its feet. Ask the kids if the bird is a climber, a swimmer, a runner, a walker, a predator, or a "perching" bird.

While you're out walking, you can also look at bird beaks. See "Fill the Bill" on page 29 for information about different kinds of bird beaks and what they do.

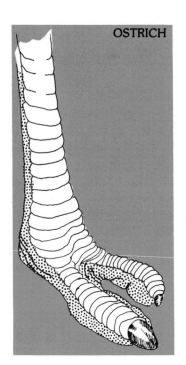
OSTRICH

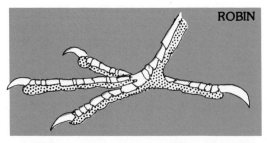
ROBIN

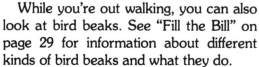
WOODPECKER

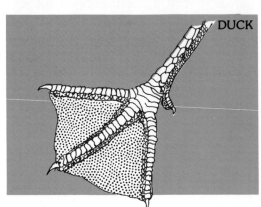
DUCK

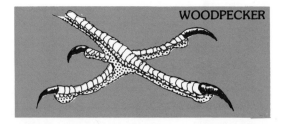
OWL

Fill the Bill

Demonstrate some ways different beaks are adapted to getting different foods.

Objective:
Describe five different types of beaks and explain how each is adapted to feed on different foods.

Ages:
Intermediate and Advanced

Materials:
- *copies of page 37*
- *3 eyedroppers or straws*
- *4 pairs of chopsticks*
- *3 nutcrackers or pliers*
- *2 large scoops or slotted spoons*
- *3 strainers*
- *3 envelopes or small fishnets*
- *3 forceps or tweezers*
- *3 tongs*
- *small log*
- *popcorn or tiny marshmallows*
- *rice*
- *puffed rice*
- *2 aquariums or other large containers*
- *fake worms or grapes*
- *oatmeal*
- *stemmed cherries*
- *tall, thin vase*
- *large saucepan*
- *walnuts or other nuts*
- *Styrofoam chunks*
- *string*

Subject:
Science

It would be impossible for a hummingbird to gobble up a mouse. And it would be just as impossible for a hawk to slurp up some nectar from a flower. Each type of bird has a special beak and tongue adapted to eating a certain type of food. In this demonstration your group can find out which beaks are best for tearing, scooping, cracking, and picking by going to different stations you've set up and trying to find out which tools go with which types of "food."

First talk about some different bird beaks to get the kids thinking about how beaks help birds survive. Here are some examples of birds and beaks you can talk about:

- **Hummingbirds** have long hollow beaks that they use to probe flowers for nectar. The beak protects the tongue which slurps up the nectar.
- **Curlews, godwits, kiwis, and snipes** have very long beaks that they use to probe for worms, crustaceans, and other small creatures in mud and water.
- **Cardinals, sparrows, grosbeaks, and other finchlike birds** have very short, conical beaks. These beaks are very strong and can break open tough seeds.
- **Spoonbills and pelicans** have long, flattened or pouchlike beaks that they use to scoop up fish and other aquatic creatures.
- **Flamingos and some ducks** have bills that act like strainers to filter tiny plants and animals from the water. (Only certain kinds of ducks are filter feeders.)
- **Nighthawks, whip-poor-wills, swifts, and swallows** have large, gaping mouths that act like nets to trap insects. These birds catch insects on the wing.
- **Warblers** have small, sharp, pointed beaks for picking insects from leaves, logs, and twigs.
- **Toucans** have very long, thick beaks for reaching out and plucking fruit from trees.

SETTING UP THE DEMONSTRATIONS

You'll need to set up eight different stations, each with a special type of "food" that fits one of the eight different types of beaks we've described. And at each station you will need three different tools—one that fits the food and two that don't fit so well. Also have a sign at each station that tells what type of food is represented. (For example, have a sign that says "nectar" at Station #1, one that says "worms in the mud" at Station #2, and so on.)

Here's a list of food and tools for each station. (The * indicates the tool that best fits the food.)

Station #1: Water in a tall, thin vase to represent nectar in a flower. (hummingbirds)
tools: eyedropper or straw*
        envelope or small fishnet
        large scoop or slotted spoon

Station #2: Large saucepan filled with dry oatmeal, with grapes on the bottom to represent worms buried in the mud. You can use fake rubber worms instead of grapes, if you can find some. (curlews, godwits, kiwis, and snipes)
tools: chopsticks*
        nutcracker
        strainer

Station #3: Whole walnuts or other nuts to represent seeds with hard coverings. (sparrows, cardinals, grosbeaks, and other finchlike birds)
tools: nutcracker or pliers*
        tongs
        chopsticks

Station #4: Styrofoam chunks floating in an aquarium filled with water to represent fish and other aquatic animals. (spoonbills and pelicans)
tools: large scoop or slotted spoon*
        eyedropper or straw
        chopsticks

(continued next page)

Station #5: Puffed rice in an aquarium filled with water to represent tiny aquatic plants and animals. (flamingos and some ducks)

tools: strainer*
forceps or tweezers
tongs

Station #6: Popcorn or tiny marshmallows tossed in the air (which must be caught while in the air) to represent flying insects. (nighthawks and whip-poor-wills)

tools: envelope or small fishnet*
forceps or tweezers
chopsticks

Station #7: Rice spread on a log to represent caterpillars and other insects. (warblers)

tools: forceps or tweezers*
envelope or small fishnet
nutcracker or pliers

Station #8: Cherries hanging from a string to represent fruit hanging from a branch. (toucans)

tools: tongs*
eyedropper or straw
strainer

DOING THE DEMONSTRATIONS

Pass out a copy of page 37 to each person. Divide the group into eight teams and start each team at a different station. Explain that there will be three different tools at each station, each of which represents a different type of bird beak function. Each group must decide which tool would most efficiently get the food at each station. (They should decide by trying out the different tools.) Once they pick the best tool, they should write the name of the tool on their Copycat Pages in the appropriate square. (You might want to set a time limit at each station to keep things moving.) Underneath the squares are pictures of different birds and their beaks. On the line under each picture, they should write the number of the square that represents the correct beak. For example, they should write "8" on the line under the toucan.

After the activity, discuss beak adaptations in general. Explain that many birds, after millions and millions of generations, have evolved very specialized beaks (beaks that can eat only one certain type of food). Ask the group how specialized beaks can help some birds stay alive. (A bird with a specialized beak can often eat a type of food that no other bird can eat.) Then ask how a specialized beak might hurt a bird. (If the bird's habitat changes and its food is no longer available, the bird might die because it can't eat anything else.) Explain that some birds, such as crows, have very versatile beaks. Crows can eat fruits, nuts, berries, dead animals, and even fish and small rodents. If one type of food is not available, they can always eat something else.

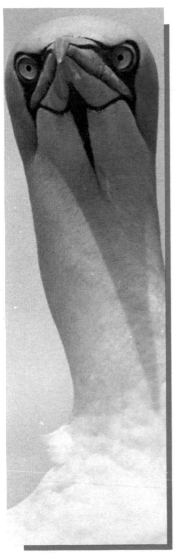

Leonard Lee Rue III   gannet

Fantasy Island

Read about a tropical island and describe two birds that might live there.

Objectives:
Define adaptation *and* niche. *Describe the relationship between habitat and adaptation.*

Ages:
Intermediate and Advanced

Materials:
- *copies of page 40*
- *drawing paper*
- *crayons or colored pencils*

Subjects:
Reading, Creative Writing, and Science Science

ne way for children to understand how niches, adaptations, and habitats all fit together is to have them create fantasy birds and describe the adaptations, niches, and habitats of their made-up birds. In this activity we've provided habitat background, but the kids have to think up the birds, adaptations, and special niches.

Pass out copies of page 40 and have each person read about the island of Aviana. Explain that this is just a very brief description of the habitats on the island, as well as some of the plants and animals that live there. There are many other creatures that live on the island, including many types of birds. Tell the children they should each pick one of the habitats (sandy beach, sandy forest, swampy forest, or field) and describe it in more detail. Then have them describe two birds that live in the habitat they have chosen. Each of the birds should have a different niche. (They might eat at different times, nest in different places, eat different foods, hunt in different ways, or migrate at different times.)

Tell the kids to explain how their birds are especially adapted to the habitat they've described. You can have them write about what, when, and how the birds eat; where they nest; what they use to build their nests; whether or not they migrate and, if they do, where they go and why; and so on. When they finish writing about their birds, have them draw a picture showing the habitat and the two birds they've described. Make sure they draw details of special adaptations the birds have for staying alive.

Afterward, have each person hold up his or her picture and talk about how each of the two birds is adapted to its habitat. Compare the different niches and adaptations that everyone came up with and then talk about some of the special adaptations of birds living in your area.

Migration Models

Make a model of the path of a migrating bird.

Objective:
Describe the migration routes of several different birds.

Ages:
Intermediate and Advanced

Materials:
- *modeling clay or homemade dough (see recipe in activity)*
- *tempera paints (optional)*
- *toothpicks or pushpins*
- *yarn*
- *cardboard or poster board*
- *chalkboard or easel paper*
- *copies of page 38 (optional—a maze for younger children)*

Subjects:
Science, Crafts, and Geography

Bird migration has mystified people for ages. But even though there's still a lot we don't know about it, scientists have managed to put some of the pieces of the migration puzzle together. For example, through bird-banding projects and other research, ornithologists have been able to find out where different birds spend the winter. And they've been able to track the general paths different species use to get to their destinations.

In this activity your kids can plot some of the different routes migrating birds take by building their own migration models out of clay or dough and using the sample migration data we provide. But before they begin, lead a discussion about migration and some of the ways scientists study it.

First explain that, in general, birds migrate to their wintering grounds along certain paths. The paths migrating birds follow generally depend on where the birds start from. For example, a flock of robins in Minnesota might fly along the Mississippi River to reach their wintering grounds, while a flock in Maine might fly along the East Coast. You can also talk about how birds are banded. (See "Band That Bird," *Ranger Rick,* Sep 84, pages 26-31.)

After talking about migration, write down each of the sets of "make-believe" data (on pages 33-34) on a separate piece of paper. Divide the kids into groups of two or three and explain that each group will be responsible for making a model of the migration path of a particular bird. Then pass out one of the sets of data to each group. Tell the kids that the migration paths these data represent are actual migration paths that researchers and banders have discovered. (For simplicity, each set of data is based on an individual, hypothetical bird.) Also explain that not all migrating birds fly as far as others of the same species. For example, our sample data of the peregrine falcon track a peregrine from its breeding grounds in Greenland all the way to its wintering

("continued on page 32")

WHAT'S ON THE MENU

Here's a rundown of some of the foods you can "serve" at your feeding station.

• **Seeds**—Seeds are food for many birds and are usually available in prepackaged mixes in grocery stores, garden supply shops, hardware stores, agricultural supply stores, and some nature centers. You can fill your feeders with these mixes or buy the different types of seeds individually and create your own mixes. (Keep in mind that some prepackaged mixes contain certain kinds of seeds that are "unpopular" with many birds.) Here are a few examples of some different types of seeds and the birds they attract:

Millet is eaten by doves, finches, sparrows, and many other birds. There are many different types of millet. Common, or proso, millet has wide appeal—especially the white variety.

Sunflower seeds are a favorite of grosbeaks, cardinals, chickadees, and many other birds.

Safflower seeds are not quite as "popular" as sunflower seeds, but cardinals and some other birds will eat them.

Niger ("thistle") seeds attract goldfinches, redpolls, pine siskins, and some other types of finches. (These seeds are best served in a hanging feeder. They don't "work well" on platform feeders because they're very light and can blow away easily.)

• **Grains**—You can spread corn, oats, wheat, and other grains on the ground, put them on a platform feeder, or mix them with other seeds and put them in a hanging feeder. (Grains usually make up a large portion of any commercial birdseed mix, and some are available separately in agricultural supply stores and other stores that sell birdseed.)
Note: Make sure you do not use grains that have been treated for planting. Some are coated with chemicals that are harmful to birds.

• **Suet**—Woodpeckers, chickadees, nuthatches, and titmice are all suet eaters. Many grocery stores and butcher shops will sell suet for next to nothing (and some even give it away). To serve suet, put it in a mesh onion bag and hang the bag from a tree. You can also spread suet on tree branches, put it in a suet log (see the last suggestion under "A Quick Look at Other Feeders"), or buy a special wire suet basket. You can also grind suet up or melt it down, mix it with seeds or grains, then put the mixture in a foil pan.

• **Nuts**—You can include almost any unsalted, shelled nuts at your feeding station. Just break the nuts into small pieces and put them on the ground or a platform feeder. You can also use peanut butter—either by itself or mixed with suet or seeds.

• **Fruits**—Orioles, tanagers, mockingbirds, and others like to eat fruits. Try anchoring orange halves to a tree branch or nailing them to a platform feeder. You can also cut apples, bananas, dates, or other fruit into small pieces and spread them out on a platform feeder. Raisins are another favorite—especially if they've been softened. (You can soften raisins by steaming them or letting them soak in water for a while.) A lot of birds will eat coconut too, but remember: PROVIDE FRESH COCONUT ONLY. Dried, packaged coconut can swell in a bird's stomach and kill it.

TIPS AND TRICKS FOR FEEDING

• Put the feeders in places that are protected from the wind and that have lots of cover nearby.

• Plant trees and shrubs that provide food for the birds. Contact your state Soil Conservation Service office for information about the best plants for your area. (Look in the phone book under Government, U.S. Department of Agriculture.)

• Place only the amount of food in a feeder that can be eaten within a few days.

• Keep feeding areas clean by raking up spilled seeds and grains periodically and wiping off messy feeders.

• Use only fresh, clean, dry seeds and grains in your feeders.

• Provide water at your feeding station by setting up a simple saucer birdbath. Use a clay saucer that is at least 24 inches (60 cm) in diameter. Set the saucer on a low tree stump or right on the ground and fill it with 1½ inches (4 cm) of water. (Clean and refill the birdbath every few days.)

SEASONAL TREATS

• *Trim a Tree for the Birds*
Decorate an evergreen tree for the birds

• *Make a No-Scare Scarecrow for the Birds*
have them scatter seeds, bread crumbs, bits of fruit and other bird treats on the

Have the kids build a scarecrow using corn husks, straw, or newspaper stuffed into old clothing. Attach the scarecrow to a wooden post or fence and set it near a window so the kids can watch. Every day, assign a group of children to "fill up" the scarecrow. Have them scatter millet, sunflower seeds, and cracked corn on the ground, as well as on the scarecrow's shoulders, arms, and hat. They can also stick raisins, coconut, dry cereal, and peanut butter on the scarecrow or hang pine cones rolled in peanut butter or suet from its head for "bushy" hair.

by stringing popcorn, toasted oat cereal, and stale doughnuts and hanging the lines on trees. Make ornaments using scooped out oranges and grapefruits, gourds, and coconuts filled with peanut butter, suet, or other bird treats.

Dress Up a Snow Sculpture for the Birds

Have the kids make a snowperson or some type of animal snow sculpture. Then sculpture. For example, on the snowperson, they could hang peanut butter pine cones from its hat, stick raisins and peanuts on its face for its eyes, nose, and mouth, and hang a necklace of stale doughnuts around its neck.

Make a Valentine for the Birds

Trace a heart on a piece of paper and cut it out. Then place the heart on a piece of stale bread and cut around the edges of the heart. Brush on egg white and sprinkle on some birdseed. Then hang the heart from a tree.

FOOD FOR THOUGHT

Divide the group into four or five teams and have each team think up a feeding experiment, using a homemade feeder and different types of bird food. Explain that each team must first come up with a hypothesis, or proposition, they want to test.

Here are some examples:
- Hummingbirds prefer red sugar water over other colors.
- Woodpeckers prefer suet rolled in birdseed over plain suet or suet mixed with oats.
- Tray feeders get used more if they are close to bushes, trees, or other natural shelter.
- Doves prefer blue or green cracked corn to yellow or red cracked corn. (Just soak the corn in food coloring for a few minutes, then let it dry before putting it out.)
- A feeding station with many different kinds of food will attract a larger variety of birds than a feeding station with just one type of food.
- Most birds feed more in the morning than in the afternoon.
- Seed-eating birds prefer a wild birdseed mix of 65% sunflower seeds, 20% cracked corn, and 15% millet, compared to 100% sunflower seeds.
- More birds will feed from a green feeder than from a red feeder of the same design that contains the same type of seed.

Tell the teams they will need to design their experiments so they can test their hypotheses. That means they must set up a system that will allow them to record their data accurately. For some experiments, they can weigh the food before they put it out on the feeder and then again at the end of each day. For other experiments, they can set up one type of feeder in three different areas or use a feeder that is divided into equal-sized compartments—each filled with a different color or type of food.

Have each team keep a data book to record the data they collect. Remind them to write with pencils or ballpoint pens (some pen ink runs when it gets wet) and label and date all their entries.

When the experiments are completed have each team write up a report explaining their experiment and the results. Then have each team make a presentation to the rest of the groups explaining what they did, how the results supported or disproved their hypothesis, and some of the reasons that the results might not be accurate. Here are some questions you can ask each team:
- What were some of the problems you had in designing your experiment and collecting the data?
- What might you have done differently?
- Did the results support your hypothesis? Why?
- How might you have made errors? (By not weighing the food accurately, not keeping an accurate record of the birds that visited the feeder, not taking the weather and other factors into consideration, and so on.)

TAKE A BIRD TO LUNCH

Setting up a feeding station is a great way to watch birds. Here are a few ideas for how to make some simple feeders using inexpensive materials you can find around the house. On the back, we've also included a few activity ideas you might want to try.

Once you set up a feeding station, it'll take the birds a little while to know it's there. But as soon as they find it, they'll keep coming back as long as you keep it stocked with food. For more bird feeding ideas, check the bibliography on page 63.

A PLASTIC JUG FEEDER

Materials:

- plastic milk or juice bottle with screw-on lid (make sure it's clean and dry)
- nail or other sharp object for punching holes in the bottle
- sharp scissors
- wooden dowel, 3/16" (5 mm) wide and about 9" (23 cm) long
- jar lid, 2" (5 cm) in diameter
- wire clothes hanger
- wire cutters

1. Trace the outline of the jar lid onto opposite sides of the plastic jug, at least 1½" (4 cm) from the bottom. Use sharp scissors to cut out the circles.

2. To make a perch, use the nail to poke a hole ½-1" (1.3-2.5 cm) under each circle. Insert the dowel so that it passes through one hole, through the jug, and out the hole on the other side.

3. Poke several small holes in the bottom of the jug so rainwater will drain out.

4. Cut a clothes hanger in two places with the wire cutters (see diagram A). Each cut should be at least 4" (10 cm) from the base of the hook. Bend the hanger so it looks like diagram B.

5. Use the nail to poke a hole about 1" (2.5 cm) from the bottle's top. Do the same on the other side of the bottle, opposite the first hole.

6. Push the ends of the hanger into the holes. Adjust the hanger so that the feeder hangs evenly and the ends of the hanger don't slip out of the holes.

7. Screw the lid on the bottle. Then fill your feeder and hang it up.

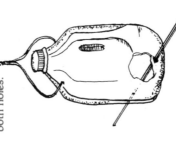

Push perch through both holes.

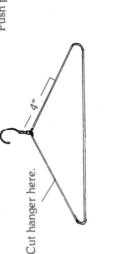

Diagram A

Cut hanger here.

4"

Diagram B

Bend hanger to this shape.

A PLATFORM FEEDER

Materials:

- flat board, at least 12" (30 cm) square
- 4 thin pieces of wood, each about 2" (5 cm) wide and as long as one side of the flat board
- tall post and post-hole

1. Drill several holes in the board for drainage.

2. Cut the thin pieces of wood into lengths to match each side of the board. Nail or glue them in place (see diagram).

3. Nail the feeder to the top of an old

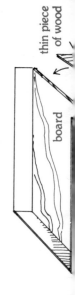

board

thin piece of wood

• digger (optional)
• nails or waterproof glue

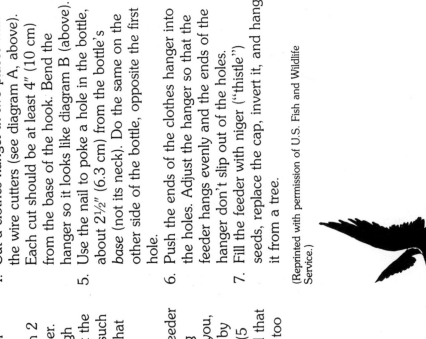

Glue to board.

post

stump or sink a post into the ground and nail the platform on top of it. Place the seeds, grains, or other food directly onto the board.

SODA BOTTLE THISTLE FEEDER

Materials:
• large plastic soft drink bottle (liter size)
• 3 or 4 wooden dowels, each 3/16" (5 mm) wide and about 8" (20 cm) long
• X-acto knife
• nail or other sharp object for punching holes in the bottle
• wire clothes hanger
• wire cutters

1. Wash the bottle and remove the label and colored base.

2. To make a perch, use a nail to punch 2 holes in the bottle, opposite each other. Insert a dowel so that it passes through one hole, through the bottle, and out the hole on the other side. Make 3 or 4 such perches, alternating the positions so that all sides of the bottle are used.

3. Now you're ready to cut the feeding holes. (Remember that the finished feeder will hang with the bottle's neck facing *down*.) With the neck facing toward you, use an X-acto knife to cut a 1/4" long by 1/8" wide (6 × 3 mm) hole about 2" (5 cm) above each perch. Keep in mind that the seeds will fall out if the holes are too big.

4. Cut a clothes hanger in two places with the wire cutters (see diagram A, above). Each cut should be at least 4" (10 cm) from the base of the hook. Bend the hanger so it looks like diagram B (above).

5. Use the nail to poke a hole in the bottle, about 2½" (6.3 cm) from the bottle's *base* (not its neck). Do the same on the other side of the bottle, opposite the first hole.

6. Push the ends of the clothes hanger into the holes. Adjust the hanger so that the feeder hangs evenly and the ends of the hanger don't slip out of the holes.

7. Fill the feeder with niger ("thistle") seeds, replace the cap, invert it, and hang it from a tree.

A QUICK LOOK AT OTHER FEEDERS

Here are a few other ideas for some easy feeders you can make:

• Tie a piece of string around a pine cone. Fill the spaces in the pine cone with suet, peanut butter, or a mixture of suet, peanut butter, and birdseed. Hang your pine cone feeder by tying the string to a branch.

• Fill foil dishes, empty margarine tubs, or the skins of orange or grapefruit halves with seeds or suet. Use wire or string to hang the feeders from a tree.

• String unshelled peanuts, popcorn, and/or berries together and drape them over tree branches.

• If hummingbirds live in your area you can attract them to your schoolyard or nature center with a nectar feeder. For instructions on how to make a simple nectar feeder, see "Invite a Hummer to Lunch," *Ranger Rick*, June 1985, pages 13-14.

• Nail metal bottle caps to a log and fill the caps with peanut butter or suet. Hang the log from a tree with wire or string.

grounds in Brazil. But a real-life peregrine may or may not go that far. It could, for example, start out in Greenland and stop for the winter somewhere along the coast of North Carolina. And a peregrine that spent the summer in North Carolina might fly to Central America for the winter.

To make the models, first have each group outline North and South America on a cardboard or poster board surface, following a rough outline that you've drawn

Bruce Norfleet

on the blackboard or large piece of paper. (Emphasize that they should draw a *rough* outline, leaving out the boundaries of states and countries. The outline will be filled in with dough or clay.) The maps can be as big or small as you want them to be, but anything smaller than what will fit on an 8½ x 11" piece of paper might be difficult to work with.

Have the kids mold landmarks such as the Appalachian and Rocky Mountains, the Mississippi and Colorado Rivers, the Great Lakes, and any other landforms and bodies of water you want them to include. (Depending on their data, they may also need to mold islands such as Cuba and Puerto Rico.) If the kids use homemade dough to make their maps, they can paint their mountains, lakes, and rivers with tempera or poster paints when the dough is dry. (It will take a day or two to dry.) If they use modeling clay, they can add different colors of clay to form the geographical features. You might also have the kids add miniature paper trees here and there. And they can paint in the Atlantic and Pacific Oceans on the poster board or cardboard.

Next have the kids plot their data onto their maps by pushing a toothpick or pushpin into the places on their maps that correspond to each bit of data. (If the kids make their maps with homemade dough, they will need to push the toothpicks or pins in while the dough is still wet.) For coastal points, the kids can mount their toothpicks or pins in a small bit of clay in the "ocean." They won't be able to mark the exact locations of the data points, but tell them to try to be as accurate as they can be. Keep maps handy so the kids can refer to them while they work.

Once the dough is dry, have the kids connect their data points by tying a piece of yarn on one of the end points, wrapping it around the toothpicks or pushpins in between, and then tying it to the other end point. Have them make poster board labels for their maps (example: "Migration Path of a Bobolink"), then put the maps on display around the room.

To follow up, lead a discussion about the many dangers birds face during migration, from harsh weather conditions and predators, to people-made obstacles such as tall buildings and planes.

For younger children, pass out the maze on page 38.

Homemade Dough Recipe

Mix the following ingredients in a saucepan:

    2 cups flour
    2 tablespoons oil
    1 cup salt
    2 cups water
    4 teaspoons cream of tartar
    vanilla or peppermint flavoring (to make it smell nice)

Cook over medium heat, stirring until the mixture starts boiling or forms a ball (about 2-3 minutes). Remove from the heat and let cool until it can be handled.

Knead the dough like bread until smooth and supple. To store the dough, keep it in a plastic bag in a cool place. (Makes enough for about 3-4 maps.)

SAMPLE MIGRATION DATA

California Gull

1. Starts from its breeding grounds in the Northwest Territories, just above Alberta, Canada.
2. Stops in a farmer's field in southwestern Saskatchewan, Canada, to feed on crickets.
3. Flies for a while with a flock of Franklin's gulls in south central Idaho.
4. Spends time at a garbage dump in western Utah.
5. Is divebombed by a peregrine falcon in southwestern Nevada.
6. Feeds on scraps from a fishing boat off northern coast of Baja California peninsula.
7. Runs into a bad rainstorm several miles south of the Tropic of Cancer.
8. Meets up with more Franklin's gulls off west coast of Mexico.
9. Made it! Reaches wintering grounds off west coast of Guatemala.

Osprey

1. Starts from its breeding grounds in northwest Oregon.
2. Rides high on rising warm air above slopes of Cascade Mountains.
3. Eagle steals fish from it near San Diego, California.
4. Nearly collides with an airplane in central Mexico.
5. Flies over miles of tropical rain forest in Costa Rica.
6. Stops to rest on west coast of Columbia, South America, after crossing Gulf of Panama.

7. Runs into cold winds over the Andes in Ecuador, South America.
8. Roosts one night in central Peru, South America.
9. Made it! Reaches wintering grounds in west central Bolivia, South America.

Peregrine Falcon

1. Starts from its breeding grounds in northeastern Greenland.
2. Flies through sleet and snow along the east coast of Baffin Island, Canada.
3. Chases and captures a duck along the east coast of Labrador, Canada.
4. Nearly flies into a lighthouse on the island of Newfoundland, Canada.
5. Lands on a ship mast near the south coast of Nova Scotia, Canada.
6. Is captured, banded, and released at a banding station on the coast of southern New Jersey.
7. Is spotted by bird watchers near Cape Hatteras, North Carolina.
8. Lands on a highrise office building in Miami, Florida, and preens.
9. Stops to wait out a thunderstorm on Puerto Rico.
10. Chases and captures a parrot in eastern Venezuela, South America.
11. Made it! Reaches wintering grounds in central Brazil, South America.

Ruby-throated Hummingbird

1. Starts from its breeding grounds in New Brunswick, Canada.
2. Stops to feed at a nectar feeder in central New Hampshire.

(continued next page)

3. Almost collides with a hang glider in south central Pennsylvania.
4. Finds another nectar feeder in southwest Virginia.
5. Nearly flies into a picture window near Atlanta, Georgia.
6. Runs into rainy weather in southwest Arkansas.
7. Rests on the Yucatan Peninsula after flying more than 500 miles (800 km) across the Gulf of Mexico.
8. Is chased by a bat falcon near the northwest coast of Honduras.
9. Made it! Reaches wintering grounds in central Nicaragua.

Whooping Crane

1. Starts from its breeding grounds in the Northwest Territories, Canada.
2. Temporarily loses sight of mate in thick fog in eastern Saskatchewan, Canada.
3. Barely avoids being blown into power lines on a windy day in south central Manitoba, Canada.
4. Stops to feed with a flock of sandhill cranes in east central South Dakota.
5. Nearly shot in east central Kansas.
6. Stops to roost near Red River on the southeastern border between Oklahoma and Texas.
7. Made it! Reaches wintering grounds in southeast Texas.

Len Rue, Jr. broad-tailed hummingbird

Yellow Warbler

1. Starts from its breeding grounds in central Saskatchewan, Canada.
2. Almost becomes a sharp-shinned hawk's meal in central North Dakota.
3. Is nearly swept up in a tornado in central Kansas.
4. Flock it's migrating with joins another flock of warblers in central Mexico.
5. Roosts in El Salvador.
6. Finds a patch of trees full of juicy caterpillars in central Panama.
7. Is stalked by an ocelot in a jungle tree in western Colombia, South America.
8. Made it! Reaches wintering grounds in northern Peru, South America.

Bobolink

1. Starts from its breeding grounds in southeastern South Dakota.
2. Lands in a farm field to feed on insects in central Illinois.
3. Flock it's flying with joins up with another flock of bobolinks in southeastern Georgia.
4. Stops to feed in a rice field in eastern Cuba.
5. Its flock splits over the Caribbean Sea. (Bobolinks they joined in Georgia head off to their own wintering grounds elsewhere.)
6. Roosts in north central Brazil, South America, near the equator.
7. Stops to feed in a grain field in central Paraguay, South America.
8. Made it! Reaches wintering grounds in central Argentina, South America.

BRANCHING OUT: A FIELD TRIP

Depending on where you live, you might be able to take your group to a banding station to watch researchers capture birds, record data about them, and band them. Check with your local Audubon Society chapter or a nature center for information about banding stations in your area. (Many nature centers also give banding demonstrations on a regular basis.)

Homing in on Habitat

(continued next page)

Discuss the importance of habitat to birds and other wildlife.

Objectives:
Explain how habitat changes affect birds and other wildlife. Describe three ways people affect habitat.

Ages:
Intermediate and Advanced

Materials:
- *construction paper*
- *bulletin board*
- *thumbtacks*
- *research books*
- *yarn*

Subjects:
Science and Social Studies

What does a mallard duck do when the marsh where it's been living is filled in with soil and becomes an apartment complex? Or what happens to a pileated woodpecker when its forest home is bulldozed and becomes a shopping center? In this activity your children will get a chance to find out how habitat changes affect birds and other animals. And they can also explore their feelings about habitat changes in their community.

To lead off the activity, talk about the competing demands for land. Make a list of all the ways the land in your community is used. (for roads, farms, gardens, parks, recreation centers, houses, shopping centers, movie theaters, apartment buildings, offices, baseball fields, wildlife refuges, churches, and so on)

Then talk about the different types of habitat that exist in your area. (meadows, pine forests, deciduous forests, streams, ponds, coasts, rocky cliffs, marshes, swamps, rain forests, deserts, chaparral, and so on) Then ask your group how they think their neighborhood has changed in the last 50 years. Did a forest once grow where a field now exists? Did a field once exist where a shopping center now stands? Did a park exist where a church or school now stands? Have some areas stayed the same?

Have each person become a community detective to try to find out how things have changed. Have them talk to their grandparents, older neighbors, teachers, or other people that have lived in the community for a long time. Give the group a few days to ask questions and do research at neighborhood libraries. Then have each person report on what he or she found.

Pick out one example of a habitat change that several of the children discovered. For example, a forest might have covered the area where the school now stands. Ask the kids what types of birds might have lived in the forest that was cleared. List the different species on the board. (You can check with the Audubon Society in your area to find out more about the birds that would be found in a specific type of habitat.)

Then ask what happened to these birds. (All the birds probably flew away when the clearing began. Any nestlings would probably have been killed. A few of the species probably returned after the school was built.)

It is important for children to understand that habitat changes involve trade-offs. When a forest is cleared and a baseball field or ice-skating rink is built, people get a recreational facility that they enjoy. But most of the animals and plants that lived in the area lose their homes.

Next divide the group into teams and have each team try to come up with five reasons why birds are important to people, other animals, and to plants. (Birds provide food for people and other animals, they help spread seeds, they eat many pest insects, many are scavengers that help get rid of decaying plants and animals, they add variety and color to our lives, and so on.) Discuss the reasons each team came up with. Then ask how the needs of people and wildlife often conflict. Houses, shopping centers, schools, churches, libraries, and other structures often conflict with the need to protect habitat. Explain that when there is conflict it's usually wildlife habitat that suffers.

With older children, discuss some of the reasons for the continuing loss of habitat:

- People want a higher "standard of living"—bigger houses, more shopping centers, and more roads and other conveniences.

- Some people want to make as much money as possible and often use land as a means of doing so. Such people often don't pay attention to the wildlife needs in the area.

- Many people don't understand the needs of wildlife and why it is important to protect habitat. People ignorant of the issues often make decisions without knowing all the facts.

- In many areas, human populations are growing so fast that habitat has to be cleared to build houses and plant crops.

- As people consume more and more material goods and use more energy, habitat loss increases too. For example,

(continued next page)

many forest areas are cleared to harvest timber that will be used to make furniture, fences, pool tables, and other consumer products. Habitat is also lost or altered as oil is drilled and coal is mined. Coal and oil provide us with energy and are also used to make many consumer products, such as plastics and paint.

California condor
(Courtesy of Los Angeles Zoo)

Talk about some of these problems and the need for compromise. Ask the kids if they would be willing to change the way they live in order to protect habitat. For example, would they be willing to give up swimming at a local beach to protect seabirds or turtles that nest there? Or give up riding trail bikes if it meant that certain animal homes would be protected? Or not eat at fast food establishments that use plastic throw-away containers?

As a follow-up have each team report on one bird in the world that is in trouble because of habitat loss. (We've listed several examples.) Then make a bulletin board highlighting each of the birds chosen. (The birds we've listed are threatened or endangered because of habitat loss. In many cases houses, shopping centers, schools, churches, roads, and other people-made structures have slowly replaced forests, swamps, meadows, and other natural habitats. In other cases their habitat was taken over for grazing and farming. And habitat loss may be just one factor that has caused the population declines.)

1. Andean condor (high country along the coast of South America)
2. Bald eagle (land near seacoasts and along lakes and rivers all over North America, the island of Bermuda, and in the northeastern part of Siberia)
3. Bald ibis (rock overhangs in Morocco and Turkey)
4. Bearded vulture (mountainous areas in northern and eastern Africa and a few parts of Asia and Europe)
5. California condor (high country of southern coastal areas in California)
6. Cape Barren goose (wet, grassy areas in southern Australia)
7. Great Indian bustard (open, grassy areas in parts of India)
8. Hawaiian goose (grassy slopes on volcanoes in Hawaii)
9. Japanese crested ibis (marshes in Japan)
10. Kagu (thick forests of New Caledonia)
11. Mauritius kestrel (forest of Mauritius)
12. Owl parrot (forests and mountains in western part of New Zealand)
13. Palawan peacock pheasant (thick forests on Palawan Island in the Philippines)
14. Philippine eagle (tropical rain forests on the island of Mindanao in the Philippines)
15. Prairie chicken (open prairies of southern Canada and the central parts of the United States)
16. Seychelles kestrel (coral sand dunes on the island of Mahne in the Seychelles Islands in the Indian Ocean)
17. Splendid parakeet (semi-arid areas on the Eyre Peninsula in Australia)
18. Swinhoe's pheasant (forested mountains on the island of Taiwan)
19. Trumpeter swan (lakes, ponds, and rivers in Alaska, Idaho, Montana, Wyoming, Alberta, and British Columbia)
20. White-eared pheasant (mountain forests and alpine meadows in Tibet)
21. Whooping crane (marshy islands and lakes in parts of Texas, Idaho, and Canada)

Copycat Page

Fill The Bill

1	2	3	4
NECTAR	WORMS IN THE MUD	SEEDS	FISH AND OTHER WATER ANIMALS

5	6	7	8
TINY WATER PLANTS AND WATER ANIMALS	FLYING INSECTS	CATERPILLARS AND OTHER INSECTS	FRUIT

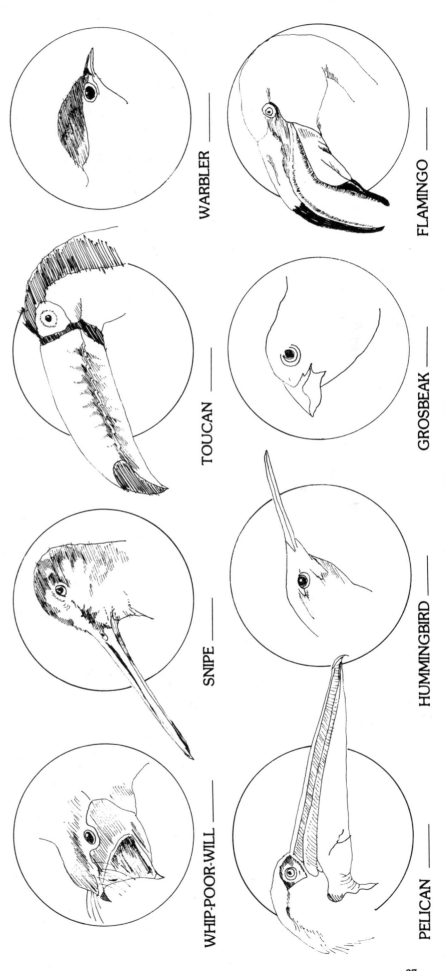

WARBLER ___

FLAMINGO ___

TOUCAN ___

GROSBEAK ___

SNIPE ___

HUMMINGBIRD ___

WHIP-POOR-WILL ___

PELICAN ___

RANGER RICK'S NATURESCOPE: BIRDS, BIRDS, BIRDS!

Help each bird find the safest path to its winter home.

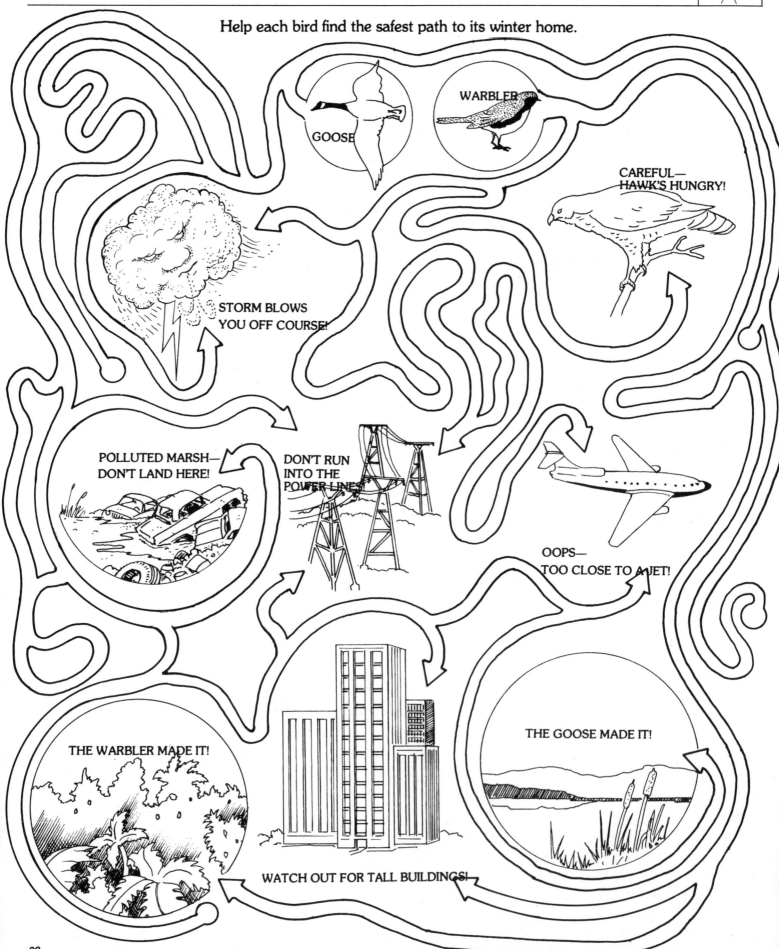

GOOSE

WARBLER

CAREFUL—
HAWK'S HUNGRY!

STORM BLOWS
YOU OFF COURSE!

POLLUTED MARSH—
DON'T LAND HERE!

DON'T RUN
INTO THE
POWER LINES!

OOPS—
TOO CLOSE TO A JET!

THE WARBLER MADE IT!

THE GOOSE MADE IT!

WATCH OUT FOR TALL BUILDINGS!

CRAZY FEET ARE NEAT

These birds all have the wrong feet! In the blank next to each bird, write the number that represents the "right" feet.

1 __

2 __

3 __

4 __

5 __

Many years ago an explorer discovered the tiny island of Aviana. Aviana was a beautiful island, with dense forests, open fields, sandy beaches, rugged cliffs, and rocky shores. Wild and colorful creatures lived on all parts of the island, and exotic wildflowers and trees, with strange fruits, seeds, and nuts, grew in each type of habitat. Here's how the explorer described the island in a book she wrote about her trip:

Large catlike predators, which the natives called dorcas, prowled the fields looking for birds and small mammals. With three twisted horns on their heads and two sharp claws on each foot, dorcas were a fierce match for their prey. Dorcas slept in the trees during the day and hunted for prey at night in the open fields of snuffgrass. They could leap three times the length of their bodies and were skilled tree climbers.

Snuffgrass was very common. It was a bright yellow weed with huge, round seed capsules that held hundreds of tiny seeds. When the capsules ripened they burst open, shooting the seeds in all directions.

Lots of weird insects lived in the fields of snuffgrass. Tiny blue caterpillars fed on the leaves and hard-backed beetles with bright red stripes lived in the seed pods. All kinds of pucos—fat grubs that tunneled in the stems of the snuffgrass—also lived in the fields.

One of the strangest plants was the bucavine. It grew in the fields of snuffgrass. Bucavines bore brightly colored fruits that were shaped like bananas but had a very hard shell. And each was filled with a sweet, honeylike juice. The flowers of the bucavine were very large and flat and each held a few drops of sweet, green nectar.

Two different kinds of forests grew on the island—one that grew in dry, sandy soil and one that grew in moist, swampy soil. The drier forest was filled with teeple trees and lufawood trees. The teeple trees had thick, syrupy sap, and super smooth bark that made them almost impossible to climb. The fruit of the teeple trees was crunchy and sweet, but the seed in the center was poisonous to many of the island creatures. The lufawood trees were very spongy. All kinds of creatures lived in the spongy branches and twigs. Slippery eelwells crawled up and down the trunk. The eelwells had sharp teeth and a slimy body, but were very tasty treats for the birds—if they could grab one and hold onto it.

In the swampy wet forest, pools of standing water surrounded clumps of huge garbon trees. The roots of the garbon trees came up through the ground and formed a maze of jungle-gym-like branches. Moosha monkeys lived among the roots and fed on the root knobs. The monkeys also fished in the water for sticky eels and turtle swanees—reptiles with long necks and sharp claws. Hard-backed worms lived in the wet, spongy soil in deep, narrow burrows. Zeepas flew over the marsh looking for prey. Zeepas were striped insects that looked like a mix of mosquito, butterfly, and wasp all wrapped up in one. Zeepas were quick fliers with delicate wings. They made their nests in the trunks of the garbon trees. Slimy mossworts grew on everything—rocks, tree trunks, and even animals' backs.

On the other side of the island, a sandy beach lined the shore. The sand was black and so were many of the creatures that lived there. Crablike animals with sharp spines lived in the sand, along with two-headed sponges, whirlyfish (fish that could sail like a Frisbee), pocket rebas (tiny mammals that tunneled in the sand), and many other creatures.

KEEPING FIT AND STAYING ALIVE

If you were a turkey vulture and you found yourself cornered, face to face with a hungry predator, what would you do? You'd throw up! Chances are your surprised enemy would back off pretty fast and go looking for a meal elsewhere. (If it still had an appetite, that is!)

Like other animals, birds have evolved a lot of different ways of keeping themselves alive. In this chapter, we'll talk about some of these survival techniques. But first we'll take a look at some of the ways birds take care of themselves day-to-day.

Feather Fitness

When it comes to dealing with enemies, most birds have an advantage that many other animals don't: They can usually avoid danger just by flying away from it. And since flying is a major key to survival for most birds, keeping the feathers in good working order is an important part of their everyday lives. Here are some of the ways birds keep their feathers "fit":

Preening: If you've ever owned a pet parakeet or other bird, you've probably noticed how much time it spent "picking" at its feathers—pulling them through its bill, nibbling them, and fluffing them out. This is called *preening,* and it's a major part of most birds' daily routines. When a bird preens, it's cleaning its feathers—removing dirt and parasites such as mites and lice. Preening also helps to "zip together" feather barbs that have separated. (See page 13 for more background information on feathers.)

Many birds also spread oil on their feathers when they preen. The oil, secreted by a special gland near the base of the tail, helps to keep birds' feathers water-repellent.

Anting is a special kind of preening in which a bird either rubs ants into its feathers with its bill or stands on an anthill and lets the ants crawl through its feathers. Jays, robins, sparrows, and many other songbirds "ant." Ornithologists aren't sure what the purpose of anting is, but many believe that certain chemicals ants produce might kill or discourage parasites such as lice and mites. Occasionally some birds will "ant" with other things besides ants, such as other insects, certain berries and other fruits, mothballs, and even smoldering cigarette butts.

Bathing: Many birds bathe before they preen. But not all birds take their baths in water. Instead, some flutter and flap in dusty soil.

Taking a bath in water helps birds stay clean, of course. And in hot weather a dip in a puddle or birdbath probably helps birds cool off. But what purpose do *dust baths* serve? Ornithologists don't know for sure, but many think dust baths might help increase the insulating capacity of feathers. And some believe they might help get rid of lice, mites, and other parasites.

Molting: Once or twice a year (and sometimes more often) all birds *molt,* or replace their old, worn feathers with new ones. Many birds molt right after the breeding season and before they migrate south. During this molt they usually lose and replace all of their feathers. At other times of the year—just before the breeding season, for example—some birds go through a partial molt. Many songbirds, herons, and others grow colorful breeding feathers and special courtship plumes during this molt.

While they're molting, most birds lose only a few feathers at a time. These feathers usually are shed from opposite sides of the bird's body simultaneously. That way the bird won't be thrown off balance when it flies. *(continued next page)*

Dealing With Danger

Here are some of the ways birds protect themselves from predators and other dangers:

Birds of a Feather: For most birds, "flocking together" is an important part of life. Birds may gather in flocks to nest, feed, migrate, or roost—usually with their own kind but sometimes with other species. Only a few kinds of birds, such as some hawks and owls, live alone most of their lives.

Safety in numbers is one of the main reasons that birds flock. It's hard for a predator to single out any one animal if that animal is part of a group. So the chance of any one bird being attacked if it's part of a flock is less than if the bird is by itself.

Freezing: A rowdy flock of songbirds, feeding in a treetop, can instantly become still when a hawk passes overhead. That's because the songbirds, catching sight of the hawk (or maybe even just its shadow), have "frozen." Since many hawks and other predators key in on movement, freezing is one way birds can avoid becoming a hungry animal's meal.

Sounding the Alarm: "Watch out—hawk's overhead!" That's one alarm message many birds communicate to each other when they spy an enemy in their area. The message, usually a short, sharp call, gets an immediate reaction from all the birds who hear it. Most will scatter into the brush, freeze, and wait for the danger to pass.

Most bird species have their own special alarm calls, but other kinds of birds living in the same habitat often understand and respond to alarm calls no matter which species makes them. What's more, many birds have different kinds of danger messages. For example, one alarm call may mean that a predator is approaching from the air, whereas another may signal that a predator is approaching from the ground.

Blending In: If you weren't looking for it (and even if you *were*), you could easily walk right past an American woodcock sitting on its forest floor nest. That's because woodcocks blend right in with leaves, grass, and other parts of their environment. The colors and patterns of their feathers help to *camouflage* them from enemies. Many owls, sparrows, rails, and some other birds also have camouflage coloration.

Camouflage changes with the seasons in the Arctic birds called ptarmigans. These ground-dwelling birds are white in the winter and are nearly invisible against snow. When they molt into their "summer coats," brown feathers replace the white ones, making the birds hard to see against the brown grasses and shrubs that they live among.

Looking Big and Mean: If you can't fly away from an attacker for one reason or another, one way to try to get rid of it is to intimidate it. Some birds try to intimidate enemies by making themselves look larger and more formidable than they really are. They do this by puffing out their feathers, holding out their wings, opening their bills, and sometimes making hissing sounds or other noises. If these actions aren't enough, some birds—especially those with sharp bills or talons—will try biting, jabbing, or grabbing to convince their attacker to let them alone.

Mobbing: Who ever heard of the prey attacking the predator? When birds mob birds of prey, that's just what they're doing. Mobbing occurs when a group of birds attacks a flying or perched hawk, owl, or other predator by diving at it, scolding it, and chasing it from the area. Crows, jays, other songbirds, and sometimes several different species together all take part in mobbing.

Usually the bird that's being mobbed was "minding its own business" when it was discovered by its harassers. But even though the bird may not be posing an immediate threat when it's attacked, most ornithologists consider mobbing to be a kind of defensive behavior, since it serves to drive away (and sometimes even kill) the predator.

Feather Fun

Talk about feathers and act out movements to a feather poem.

Objectives:
Describe how a feather grows. Explain why birds preen and molt their feathers.

Ages:
Primary

Materials:
* *feather*

Subject:
Science

By acting out this feather poem, your kids can learn more about how feathers grow and how they help birds. But before the kids "perform," have them sit in a circle. Pass around a feather for them to touch and look at as you explain how feathers grow, how birds preen their feathers, and how they replace old feathers through molting. (See page 13 for more about feathers.)

Then read the short poem at the right and go over the movements with the kids. After they've "rehearsed," have them try the movements a couple more times as you read the poem.

WORDS	ACTIONS
I'm a little feather nub In a bird's skin.	Crouch down with head between knees.
I'll grow and grow and grow Till I'm long and thin.	Slowly stand up and reach toward the sky.
I keep birds warm And help them fly around.	Wrap arms around body. Hold arms straight out.
But one day I'll fall out, And go sailing to the ground.	Slowly sway back and forth and gradually crouch down again.

Birds and Other Beasts

Talk about some of the ways birds and other animals are alike.

Objectives:
Name several things all animals need to survive. Give an example of a bird and another animal that have something in common.

Ages:
Primary

Materials:
* *copies of page 46*
* *pictures of birds and other animals*

Subject:
Science

What do a flock of songbirds, a herd of deer, and a school of fish all have in common? Even though these three kinds of animals are very different in a lot of ways, they all use a common survival technique: safety in numbers. In this activity your group can compare some of the ways birds and other animals are alike by looking at how various animals take care of themselves and avoid danger.

Start the activity by talking about some of the very general things birds have in common with all other animals. For example, birds—like insects, fish, reptiles, mammals, and every other kind of animal—must eat to stay alive. And all animals need a place to live, whether that place is in a forest, a marsh, a meadow, or a river. Point out that, because birds and other kinds of animals have many of the same needs, they often react to certain situations in the same ways.

Next pass out copies of page 46 and lead a discussion about some of the similar ways birds and other animals protect themselves and keep themselves in good physical condition. Begin by having the kids look at the first picture on the left side of the page. Explain that this marsh bird, called a bittern, has a special way of hiding from hungry animals: It points its long, thin neck and bill toward the sky. This makes the bittern blend in with the long thin reeds, cattails, and other marsh plants it lives among.

Now have the kids point to two other animals on the page that can hide from enemies by blending in with their surroundings. (The insect that looks like a leaf is a type of katydid and the fish that resembles coral is a trumpetfish.) Explain that many kinds of insects look like leaves, sticks, thorns, and other things that a bird or other animal would not want to eat. And some fish, such as the trumpetfish in the picture, hold their long, thin bodies upside down so

(continued next page)

they look like coral, water plants, and other things that a meat-eating fish would not be interested in.

As the children look at the second picture, explain that bathing helps birds get rid of pests such as mites and lice. And just like people, birds may cool themselves off on warm days by getting wet. Have the kids point to the other "bathers" on the page. (the child and the cat)

Even though a bird's feathers are strong, they eventually wear out—like anything else that gets used a lot. Have the kids look at the third picture while you explain that birds *molt*—shed old feathers and grow new ones—once or twice a year (and occasionally more often). Animals with fur often *shed* their hair, just as birds molt their feathers. Ask the kids which of the animals on the page is probably shedding. (the dog that's being brushed)

Now ask the kids to think about birds they've seen outside. Do they usually see just one bird by itself or a lot of birds together? Talk about the fact that most birds spend a lot of time with others of their kind. Sometimes a large group, or flock, of birds will gather to feed, sleep, nest, or migrate. One important reason that birds flock is that they are safer in a group than they would be by themselves. That's because a bird is less likely to be attacked by a hungry animal when it's part of a group.

Safety in numbers applies to other animals too. What other animal groups can the kids point to on the Copycat Page? Ask if anyone can say what these two kinds of groups are called. (school of fish, herd of deer)

To wrap up your discussion about how birds and other animals survive and stay healthy, you might want to talk about some specific features that certain birds and other animals share. For example, show the kids a picture of a lion and an eagle and ask the group how the two are alike. (Both animals hunt other animals for food.) Point out that lions, eagles, and many other *predators* have sharp claws on their feet for catching their *prey*. Porpoises and penguins are also alike. Like porpoises, penguins spend a lot of time in the water. The penguins' flipperlike wings, similar to a porpoise's flippers, help them move quickly through the water.

Bird Behavior Bingo

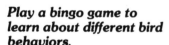

Play a bingo game to learn about different bird behaviors.

Objective:
Describe two different bird behaviors and how they help birds survive.

Ages:
Primary and Intermediate

Materials:
- *copies of page 47*
- *pieces of cardboard (about 8½ x 11" [21 x 28 cm])*
- *scissors*
- *markers*
- *paste or glue*
- *plastic lamination or clear contact paper (optional)*
- *grease pencils (optional)*

Subject:
Science

Play Bird Behavior Bingo to get your kids outside with the birds. It's a fun way to learn to observe while becoming familiar with how birds behave.

First pass out copies of page 47. Have the kids make their own bingo boards by cutting out the bingo squares and pasting or gluing them in a different order on a piece of cardboard.

You can use the boards as is or cover them with clear contact paper to make them stronger and reusable. Just have the children mark on the "permanent" boards with grease pencils so you can wipe the marks off after every game.

Next take the group on a bird hike. (Make sure they all bring along their boards and something to write with.) Whenever they spot (or hear) one of the behaviors pictured on their boards, have them mark the pictures with an X. Then talk about the behavior. For example, if you saw a bird preening, you could discuss how and why birds preen. You could also talk about birds' oil glands and parasites.

Occasionally you may run across birds that are doing two things at once. For example, you could see a flock of pigeons feeding. If this happens you can either have the kids mark both pictures (in this case, the feeding and flocking squares) or just one, depending on how long you want your hike to last.

The first person to mark three pictures in a row, either across, down, or diagonally, is the winner. (If you make reusable boards, you may want to vary the game a little by making the requirements different each time. For example, "bingo" could be all four corners, an L-shape, a T-shape, a Z-shape, or an I-shape. Or you could have the kids try to mark all nine of their pictures.)

Molt the Duck

Answer questions to discover the colors of a molted bird.

Objectives:
Define molting. *Give several examples of ways birds take care of their feathers.*

Ages:
Intermediate

Materials:
- *copies of pages 48 and 49*
- *crayons or colored markers*
- *pictures of birds in young and adult plumages and in winter and breeding plumages (optional)*
- *pictures of young and adult mallard ducks (optional)*

Subjects:
Science and Art

Without feathers, birds would not be birds. Besides being unique in the animal world, feathers help birds fly, attract a mate, and stay warm. That's why it's essential that birds take good care of their plumage.

To test and reinforce your group's knowledge of how birds keep their feathers in good shape, try this molting activity.

scarlet tanager

Start the activity by talking a little about feather "fitness" in general, using the background information on pages 41-42. You might also want to show the kids some "before and after" molting pictures. For example, discuss the fact that many birds have different feather colors and patterns when they're young than they do when they're adults. Show pictures of immature and adult bald eagles and point out that young bald eagles are basically brown all over with some white patches here and there. Not until they're at least four years old do they molt into their adult plumage of a dark brown body and white head and tail.

You can also talk about birds that molt into bright colors or grow special feathers to attract a mate. For example, some male goldfinches and tanagers molt from their drab winter colors into bright yellows and reds during the breeding season. And many egrets grow long graceful plumes during this time.

After your discussion, pass out copies of pages 48 and 49 to each person. Have the kids work alone or in teams to answer the questions and color the ducks. (You may want to give them some research time.) The first person or team to answer all the questions and correctly color the adult duck is the winner!

When all the kids are finished, ask them what kind of ducks they just colored. (They're both mallards.) You might want to show them pictures of young and adult male mallards so they can see how closely their crayon colors match the actual colors. (They won't be exact, but they should be pretty close.)

BIRDS AND OTHER BEASTS

1

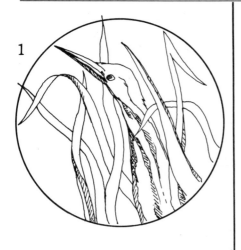

2

3

4

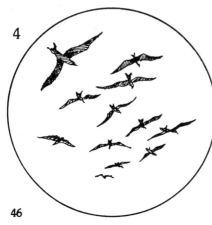

COPYCAT PAGE

BIRD BEHAVIOR BINGO

Flocking

Bathing
(in water or dust)

Feeding

Hiding

Giving an alarm call

Preening

Freezing

Singing

Flying

MOLT THE DUCK—PART 1

Use the numbers below to color this young male duck. (Leave the spaces without numbers white.)

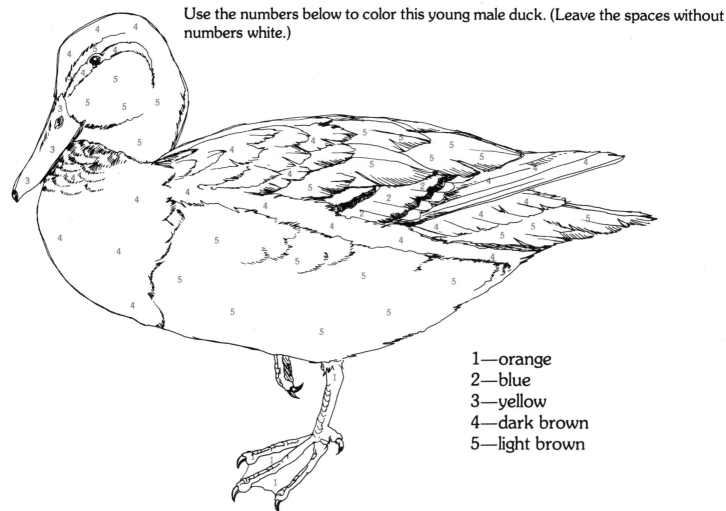

1—orange
2—blue
3—yellow
4—dark brown
5—light brown

Use the question sheet to find out what colors the duck has molted into now that it's an adult. Do you know what kind of duck this is?

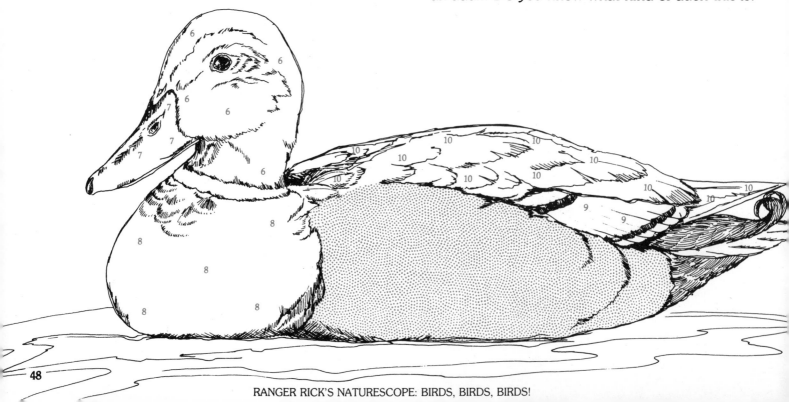

To find out what colors to make the adult duck, fill in the blanks in each group of questions below. Then unscramble the circled letters to find the duck's colors.

Color Number 6 (Make this color a dark shade.):

1. Many egrets grow special long feathers in the _ O _ _ _ _ _ _   _ _ _ _ _ O. (two words)

2. Birds _ _ OO _ their feathers by pulling them through their bills.

3. While preening, many birds coat their feathers with oil from a special O _ _ _ _.

Color Number 6 is _ _ _ _ _ _.

Color Number 7:

4. Most birds _ O _ _ at least once a year.

5. Most birds are still able to _ OO while they're molting.

6. Pests such as mites and O _ _ O sometimes live in birds' feathers.

7. Oil on a bird's feathers makes O _ _ _ _ roll off. This helps the feathers stay dry.

Color Number 7 is _ _ _ _ _ _ _.

Color Number 8 (Go over this color lightly with a brown crayon.):

8. Most _ O _ _ _ male songbirds are more brightly colored than adult female songbirds.

9. Many birds molt just before they _ _ _ O _ _ O south in the fall.

Color Number 8 is _ _ _.

Color Number 9:

10. _ O _ _ O is another word for feather.

11. Some birds take O _ _ _ _ in dust.

12. Sometimes birds spread out their wings and warm themselves in the _ O _.

Color Number 9 is _ _ _ _ .

Color Number 10 (Make this color a light shade.):

13. _ _ OO feathers are right next to a bird's body and help to keep the bird warm.

14. Since birds need water just as all animals do, a good way to attract birds to your yard is to set up a _ _ O _ O _ _.

15. A _ O _ _ _ bird's plumage is often very different from the adult's.

Color Number 10 is _ _ _ _ _ .

PEOPLE AND BIRDS

Birds have really become a big part of our lives. We eat them, use their eggs in cooking, make clothing from their feathers, sing about them, imitate them in our dance, paint pictures of them, try to fly as they do, name our kids and cars after them, keep them as pets, make up myths and stories about them, tromp all over the world to see them, and use bird-related words in our everyday speech. In fact, birds are so much a part of our lives that it's impossible to imagine what it would be like without them.

Birds not only feed us and inspire us, they also play a very important part in the world's ecology. Some eat harmful pests and weed seeds, many spread seeds, others are scavengers and feed on dead and decaying animals, and many are prey for other animals. Birds are also sensitive indicators of how healthy our environment is because they often show the effects of pollution and pesticides long before the effects show up in people or other animals.

The activities in this chapter will look at how birds have affected our lives and how we've affected their lives and created problems for them. They'll also look at ways we can help protect them.

Birds in Trouble

When Christopher Columbus came to the New World, there were over three billion passenger pigeons living in America's forests. But by 1914, there wasn't a single one left. Like the dodo, the great auk, the Labrador duck, and the heath hen, the passenger pigeon had become *extinct*.

Many birds (and other animals and plants) become extinct when they cannot adapt to changing conditions such as ice ages, volcanic eruptions, and natural competition from other species. Dinosaurs, saber-toothed cats, woolly mammoths, trilobites, and many other animals have become extinct from natural causes. But in the last 300 years, over 87 species of birds have become extinct specifically because of people's actions—not natural causes.

Here are some of the main reasons that so many birds have disappeared and why there are still so many birds in trouble today:

- **Habitat Destruction**—Draining wetlands, clearing tropical rain forests, and destroying other bird habitats are the most serious threats to bird populations today. Each year, millions of acres of bird habitat become buildings, parking lots, roads, and fields for grazing and farming.
- **Feathers, Skins, and Beaks for Sale**—Peacock, egret, and ostrich feathers; bird of paradise skins and feathers; eagle feathers and talons; ground-up hornbill beaks; and other bird "parts" have often been overcollected in the past, causing many bird populations to decline. Even with the strict laws we have today, many bird products are still sold illegally in countries all over the world.
- **Illegal Pet Trading**—Every year thousands of parrots, cockatoos, lovebirds, lorikeets, macaws, and other parrotlike birds are transported illegally from their homes in the wild and sold as pets in other countries. To smuggle them in, illegal traders often stuff them into stockings, car seats, and other concealed places. Many of these smuggled birds suffocate, starve, or die of thirst en route. And in many areas, the illegal pet traffic is threatening already endangered tropical bird populations.
- **Lead Shot Poisoning**—Many states still allow hunters to use lead shot instead of steel shot when they hunt. Scientists have shown that lead shot poisons 2-3 million waterfowl each year when the waterfowl accidentally eat the "spent" lead shot lying on the bottom of bodies of water.

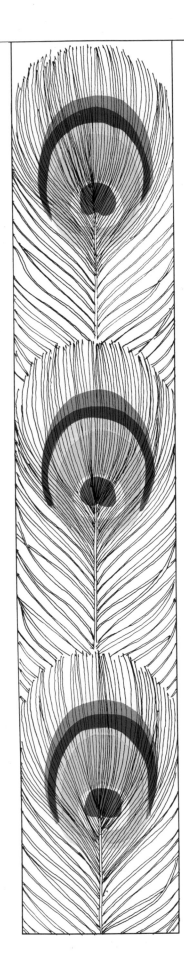

- **Rats, Cats, Pigs, and Mongooses on the Loose**—Introducing animals from one place to another can often upset the natural balance in a habitat. On many islands, introduced animals such as rats, cats, minks, pigs, and mongooses have killed ground-nesting and flightless birds and gobbled up their eggs. As a result, many of these island birds have become extinct.

  Even introduced birds can cause problems. For example, in the United States, starlings and house sparrows compete with native birds for food and nest sites, which often causes serious food and nest site shortages for bluebirds and other native species.

- **Pesticides Linger On**—DDT and other deadly pesticides have caused many bird populations to decline in the last fifty years. Eagles, hawks, and other birds of prey are especially susceptible to pesticide poisoning. When DDT was banned in the U.S. in 1972, many bird populations began to increase slowly. But DDT and other banned pesticides are still being manufactured and sold in other countries. They poison not only some of the resident birds of those countries, but also some of the migratory birds that live in those countries for part of the year. (Recent studies have also shown that DDT contamination is again on the rise in this country due to an increase in use of pesticides from other countries that use DDT.)

- **Pollution Problems**—Oil spills and chemical dumpings have killed thousands of birds, especially those living on or near water.

How to Help

Although many birds are still facing big problems and habitat is being quickly gobbled up, there are many ways people can give birds the helping hand they need. Here are some ideas:

- **Build Nesting Boxes**—Many cavity-nesting birds, such as wood ducks and bluebirds, have "bounced back" due to dedicated nesting box builders. Check the bibliography on pages 63 and 64 for books and articles about how to build nesting boxes for ducks, owls, songbirds, and other types of birds.

- **Learn More About Birds**—The more you know about birds, the more you can help them. Read up on the problems and get involved in finding solutions. You can also join a local bird club or conservation group to find out more.

- **Write Letters**—By letting your elected officials know how you feel about national and local issues, you can influence how they vote on those issues. Get involved in national issues, such as the reauthorization of the Endangered Species Act or the Clean Water Act. Or focus your attention on state and local bird issues and ways to protect habitat in your area.

- **Sponsor Projects That Help Protect Habitat**—You and your groups can raise money to support national organizations that are buying land for bald eagles, whooping cranes, wood ducks, and other birds. Or you can volunteer your time and donate money to local groups involved with habitat improvement.

- **Garden for the Birds**— You can attract more birds to your backyard or community by planting the trees, shrubs, and wildflowers that provide food and shelter for the birds that live in your area. You can also manage your land to leave protected hedgerows and dead tree "snags" for nest sites and shelter. See page 63 for books about attracting birds to your property.

Watch the Birdie

Make pretend binoculars and take a bird watching walk.

Objectives:
Describe two different kinds of birds. Name three things that can help in identifying birds.

Ages:
Primary

Materials:
- *empty toilet paper or paper towel rolls*
- *masking tape*
- *string*
- *paper and crayons*

Subject:
Science

Introduce young children to bird watching by having them "zoom in" on birds with home-made binoculars. But before you go outside, discuss some bird watching basics.

Talk about some of the birds that live in your neighborhood. Explain that different kinds of birds have different-colored body parts and have different body shapes and sizes. Different birds also have special beaks and feet, and they live in different areas.

Next pick two volunteers from the group and have them stand up front so that everyone can see them. Ask the rest of the group to compare the two children. How are they alike? (Both have hair, two legs, brown eyes, blue sneakers, and so on.) How are they different? (One has glasses and the other doesn't, one has blond hair and the other has brown hair, one is tall and the other is short, one is wearing a red shirt and the other is wearing a blue shirt, and so on.)

Explain that birds, like people, come in lots of different shapes and sizes. They might look similar from a distance, but when you get close to them, you can see that there are lots of differences between different kinds of birds.

Now have the kids make their own pretend binoculars to take with them on a bird watching walk. (The binoculars won't really work, of course, but they will help young children focus in on the birds they see.) Here's how to make them:

1. Place two paper rolls side by side. (Two toilet paper rolls work well. You can also use a paper towel roll that's been cut in half.)
2. Tape the rolls together with a long piece of masking tape.
3. Punch holes in the sides of the binoculars near the top of the rolls.
4. Tie a piece of string to the holes. Be sure the string is long enough for the binoculars to hang around the child's neck.

When you get the kids outside, have them try to spot different kinds of birds and then look at them through their binoculars. Explain that they must walk very quietly and be very still when they see a bird. Point out different shapes, colors, and sizes. When you come back inside, have the children draw pictures of the birds they saw on the walk.

National Zoological Park
Smithsonian Institution
© Smithsonian Institution

Bird Bop

Imitate the ways different birds move by dancing to different kinds of music.

Objective:
Describe some of the ways different birds move.

Ages:
Primary

Materials:
- *tape or record player and music (see activity for suggestions of kinds of music)*

(continued next page)

Soaring, hopping, strutting, climbing—these are just a few of the ways birds move. Your kids can have a lot of fun imitating bird movements by doing the "Street Pigeon Strut," the "Turkey Vulture Twirl," and other dances. It's an active way for them to become familiar with some different kinds of birds, and it'll help them recognize a few common species based on the ways they move.

Before the kids start dancing, show them pictures of the birds they'll be imitating (see next page). As you talk about each bird's movements, have the kids practice the "dance steps" we've described for each one. Then hit the music and let the kids strut, soar, step, waddle, and "hustle" like the birds.

Pigeons: These birds jerk their heads in and out as they walk. To do the "Street Pigeon Strut," have the kids form a big circle. When you start the music, have them put their hands behind their backs, bob their heads in and out, and take short, quick steps as they walk around the circle. Big band music is great for "strutting."

Turkey Vultures: The turkey vulture is a great example of a bird that can be identified by the way it flies. With its broad wings, this bird can soar for hours on pockets of rising warm air. As it soars, it holds its wings in a slight V-shape and tilts from side to side on the air currents. Have your kids imitate a turkey vulture's flight by holding their arms out in a V-shape. They can do the "Turkey Vulture Twirl" by walking in a wide circle with outstretched arms and slowly tilting their arms and bodies this way and that. Play slow, calm, "graceful" music.

Bruce Norfleet

Penguins: In the water they're graceful and fast, but on land most penguins waddle around, holding out their flippers partway for balance. Have your kids imitate penguins by holding their arms out at an angle to their bodies. As they do the "Penguin Shuffle" they can exaggerate a penguin's waddling gait by swaying back and forth and taking small steps around a circle. Ragtime music really fits the "shuffle."

Hummingbirds: When it comes to flying, hummingbirds can do a lot of things other birds can't. As it zips from flower to flower searching for nectar, a hummingbird can hover, dart up and down or from side to side, or even fly backward for short distances. To do the "Hummingbird Hustle," have the kids flap their "wings" as fast as they can. They can stand in two lines facing each other as you call out the different ways they should move. (Have them move only three or four steps each time.) Here are some examples of "commands" you can call out: *Dart to the left! Dart to the right! Hover! Fly forward! Fly backward!* Have the kids do the "hustle" to a fast piece such as Rimsky-Korsakov's "The Flight of the Bumblebee."

Sparrows: Sparrows spend a lot of time hopping around on the ground looking for food. Have your kids do the "Sparrow Hop" to the "Mexican Hat Dance" or some other rhythmic tune.

Name That Bird

Here's an activity that will help your kids learn how to identify birds. As an introduction, use the information in "What Bird Is That?" (at the end of the activity) to talk about some of the things the kids can look for when they're identifying birds. (You may want to show the kids pictures of some of the birds we've listed as examples.) Then make up a list of 16 birds found in your area. (If you need help, contact your local Audubon Society chapter or nature center or check the range maps in a field guide.) Write the name of each type of bird on a separate slip of paper and put the slips into a sack. Also write the names of all the

birds on the board or a large piece of easel paper.

Next divide your group into four teams. Have each team pick four names from the sack. (Tell them to keep the identity of their four birds a secret from the other teams.)

Then pass out a field guide to each team. (If possible, all the teams should be using the same type of field guide.) Next pass out copies of "Name That Bird" on page 57 to all the members of each team. Also give each team one extra copy of the chart. Using their field guide, have the team work together to fill in their charts. (They'll need plenty of research time.)

(continued next page)

Materials:
- pencils
- field guides
- copies of page 57
- pictures of birds (optional)
- chalkboard or easel paper

Subject:
Science

Instruct the children to fill in the charts as completely and accurately as possible. Under *How Big Is It?* they should record the bird's length in inches and centimeters and then give a comparison, using a sparrow, robin, or crow as a reference bird. For example, a bird might be bigger than a robin, but smaller than a crow. (A sparrow is about 6″ [15 cm] long, a robin is about 10″ [25 cm] long, and a crow is about 18″ [45 cm] long.) Under *Where Does It Live?* they should record the bird's habitat. For example, a bird might live in a marsh, a coniferous forest, or a meadow. On the extra chart they should fill in all of the same information except the names of the birds.

When they're finished, collect each team's extra chart and run off enough copies so that each team has a copy of the other teams' charts. (You may first want to check the legibility and accuracy of each team's chart.) Explain to the kids that the teams are going to compete against each other to see which can identify all of the birds the fastest.

Have the teams use the field guides and the information on the charts to fill in the missing names. (They can refer to the names you've written on the board or easel paper to see what the possibilities are. You might also want to hang pictures around the room of the 16 birds you're working with to give the kids some visual clues.) The first team that correctly fills in all the bird names wins.

WHAT BIRD IS THAT?

Here are some things to look for when you're trying to figure out what bird you're looking at:

Color and Field Marks—Notice the color of the bird's head, body, wings, and tail. Also notice any special patterns. Does the bird have bars on its wings, rings around its eyes, or stripes above its eyes? Check a field guide for diagrams of these and other common bird field marks.

Size and Shape—Compare the size and shape of the bird to those of other common birds. Robins, sparrows, and crows all make good "reference birds." For example, you may notice that the bird you're looking at is about the size of a robin but more slender.

Wings and Flight—You can get a good idea of what flying bird you're looking at just by noticing the shape of its wings. For example, falcons and swallows have long, pointed wings. Quails and certain hawks, on the other hand, have shorter, rounder wings.

Also pay attention to the way the bird flies. Does it fly in a straight line like a dove, or does it dip up and down like a woodpecker? Does it soar in wide circles like a vulture?

Behavior—Some birds have certain mannerisms that help distinguish them from others. For example, nuthatches, creepers, and woodpeckers all climb trees. Spotted sandpipers "teeter" as they walk, and palm warblers wag their tails.

SWIFT

HUMMINGBIRD

FALCON

ALBATROSS

GOOSE

PHEASANT

Habitat—When you're trying to identify a bird, keep in mind where the bird is—along a riverbank, on a mountaintop, or in a prairie, for example. Also keep in mind the specific place you see the bird. For example, many sparrows stay close to the ground, whereas most warblers flit around high up in the treetops.

Special Features—Don't forget to notice the obvious! For example, does the bird you're looking at have a distinctive bill, like a hawk's or hummingbird's? Does it have extra-long legs like a heron's?

A Scrapbook for the Birds

Make a scrapbook about people and birds.

Objective:
Describe three ways birds have affected people's lives.

Ages:
Intermediate and Advanced

Materials:
- *large pieces of construction paper*
- *crayons and markers*
- *magazines (for cutting out pictures)*
- *newspapers (for cutting out articles)*
- *scissors*
- *hole punch*
- *glue*
- *yarn or string*
- *reference books*
- *two pieces of cardboard (the same size as the construction paper, or a little bigger)*
- *copies of page 58*
- *chalkboard or easel paper*

Subjects:
Science, Art, and Social Studies

From the time of the first cave drawings, people have been painting birds. And they've been raising them, eating them, writing about them, and singing about them too! By making a "People and Birds Scrapbook," your group can learn about the many ways birds have affected people's lives.

We've divided the ways birds have affected people into five major categories. (See "Birds in Our Lives" at the end of the activity.) Each category is followed by several topics that relate to it.

First list all of the categories and topics on the board or a large piece of easel paper. Split your group into five teams and assign one of the categories to each team. (You may need to add or take away a team member here and there, since some categories have more topics than others.) Then give everyone a piece of construction paper. To make the scrapbook, each person will choose a topic from his or her team's category. Then he or she can either cut related photographs and articles from magazines and newspapers or draw pictures that tell about the topic. For example, one member of the Recreation Team could look for pictures about falconry, another could illustrate birding, and another could find information on birds as pets. (Some of the kids will need to do some research about their topics. Keep bird reference books handy.) Then have the kids glue their illustrations, articles, and photographs to their pages.

Give the kids some extra time to dig up some interesting facts about their topics, such as the origins of the myths under the Literature category. The teams can also add any other subheadings they can think of.

When everyone has finished his or her page, punch three holes down the left-hand side of each page. Put all the pages together, add a cardboard cover and back, and tie the "People and Birds Scrapbook" together with yarn or string. Leave the scrapbook where everyone can look through it. As your group continues learning about how birds affect people, they can add more pages.

To follow up, pass out copies of the crossword puzzle on page 58 for the kids to work on.

BIRDS IN OUR LIVES

1. *Food and Feathers*
   - chickens
   - turkeys
   - ducks and geese
   - eggs
   - quill pens
   - feather pillows, quilts, and beds
   - down vests and jackets

2. *Recreation*
   - falconry
   - birding (bird-watching)
   - bird feeding
   - pets
   - hunting
   - pigeon-racing
   - photography

3. *Literature*
   - poetry
   - fairy tales
   - myths (Phoenix, Roc, Thunderbird, Halcyon, Chinese Phoenix)
   - cartoon birds

4. *Symbols*
   - national and state symbols
   - common sayings
   - birds symbolizing ideas (dove, hawk, owl)
   - birds used in advertising

5. *Arts*
   - painting
   - sculpture
   - carving (totem poles and duck decoys)
   - songs
   - dance (ballet)
   - stamps and coins

Birds in the News

Make a bird newspaper that focuses on bird conservation and current events.

Objective:
Describe a bird-related issue currently in the news.

Ages:
Intermediate and Advanced

Materials:
- *paper and pencils*
- *newspapers*
- *magazines (optional— for cutting out pictures)*
- *glue or tape*

Subjects:
Science and Social Studies

There are many problems facing birds today, from loss of habitat to pesticide poisoning. (See background on page 51.) But there are also many people working hard to help birds survive. In this activity, your group can learn more about bird issues by keeping an eye on the news and making team newspapers.

Divide the group into teams of four or five children. Explain that each team will be making a newspaper about bird issues and bird conservation. The newspaper can be filled with items such as:
- bird-related articles cut from newspapers
- reports on birds in trouble
- interviews with people in the neighborhood who are helping to protect birds
- community bird issues
- reports on environmental problems affecting birds
- poems or stories about the problems facing birds
- pictures and stories of birds that are "bouncing back"
- habitat issues

The newspapers can have a cartoon section; an editorial page; an international, national, and local section; a good news page; and anything else, as long as it has to do with bird issues and conservation.

After all the team papers are completed, discuss some of the major issues that are in the news today. Have the children try to look at both sides of a problem and decide what they would do if they were in charge.

Then ask the group to come up with ways they could help birds (make nesting boxes, hold a "birdathon" to raise money for organizations that are helping birds, write letters to elected officials about bird-related issues, learn more about birds, become involved in community projects that can help birds, and so on).

COPYCAT PAGE

NAME THAT BIRD

BIRD'S NAME	WHAT ARE ITS COLORS AND FIELD MARKS?	HOW BIG IS IT?	WHERE DOES IT LIVE?	OTHER THINGS TO NOTICE (flight pattern, wing shape, call, special behaviors):

BIRDBRAIN CROSSWORD

Down:

1. If you think someone is not brave or daring, you might call him or her a _ _ _ _ _ _ _.
3. Statues that decorate lawns often look like this pink bird.
5. In some areas, the return of this bird is a sign that spring's on the way.
7. Miners tested for dangerous gases with this bird—now it's a popular pet.
9. The bald _ _ _ _ _ is the national emblem of the United States.
11. *The* _ _ _ _ _ is a famous poem written by Edgar Allan Poe.
13. "Silly as a _ _ _ _ _ _."
15. *The Ugly* _ _ _ _ _ _ _ _ _ is a fairy tale written by Hans Christian Andersen.
17. "Light as a _ _ _ _ _ _ _ _ _."
19. Many people eat this bird at Thanksgiving.

Across:

2. These birds carried messages during World War II.
4. _ _ _ _ _ _ _ _ are often imported illegally from South America, Asia, and Africa.
6. The _ _ _ _ _ _ _ _ _ _ _ is a fast-running desert bird that also appears in cartoons.
8. "Crazy as a _ _ _ _ _."
10. This bird's name is also the last name of a famous nurse.
12. This bird often soars for hours in search of dead animals.
14. This bird "works the night shift."
16. A scare _ _ _ _ sometimes keeps birds from eating a farmer's crops.
18. In folklore, this bird delivers human babies.
20. This bird is a symbol of peace.

CRAFTY CORNER

Here are some bird art and craft ideas you can use to complement many of the activities in the first five sections.

Avian Roly-Polys

Make wobbly bird figures out of plastic pantyhose eggs.

Ages:
Primary and Intermediate

Materials:
- *plastic pantyhose eggs (white or black)*
- *modeling clay*
- *scissors*
- *construction paper*
- *tape or glue*

Subjects:
Arts and Crafts

Your kids can make bird figures that will rock 'n' roll all day long! Give each child a plastic egg and a lump of clay (about the size of a golf ball) and have them follow these steps:

1. Open the plastic egg and press the lump of clay into the smaller half. Put the egg back together and try to make it stand up. (If it doesn't, adjust the clay inside the egg.)
2. Using the illustrations shown and pictures in reference books as guides, cut out eyes, beaks, wings, and feet for your bird.
3. Tape or glue the cut-outs onto the egg. (If you use glue, let the glue become tacky before you press the bird parts on.) Then launch your bird's rock 'n' roll career by giving it a push!

Parrot Puppets

Make parrot puppets out of household items.

Ages:
Intermediate

Materials for one puppet:
- *two small envelopes of the same size*
- *newspaper, tissue paper, or other thin paper*
- *small scrap of red felt or red paper*
- *construction paper*
- *glue*
- *stapler*
- *paint or colored markers*
- *scissors*
- *copies of the upper beak and foot patterns*

Subject:
Arts and Crafts

By following the easy steps below, your kids can make their own parrot "pals." But before they begin, pass out two envelopes to each person. Also pass out copies of the upper beak and foot patterns shown on page 60. Here's how to make a puppet:

1. **To make the head,** cut the flaps off two envelopes. Tuck one envelope inside the other with both openings facing in the same direction. Put your left hand inside the double envelope with your fingers pointing toward corner A and your thumb toward corner B. Push the fold against your right hand, flattening the fold from A to B. With the edge of your right hand, push toward your left hand at point C. Fold the envelope over your right hand as if the envelope were "biting" it. (See the steps in diagram A.) Then pinch the fold so that the envelope will stay in that position.

2. **To make the beak,** color and cut the upper beak pattern. Fold a piece of construction paper, then place the pattern on the fold, trace it, and cut it out. Glue the edges of the beak together from D to E. Then glue the beak onto the head. Color the lower beak to match the upper one (see diagram B).

3. **To make the crest,** cut strips in a 4 x 8″ (10 x 20 cm) piece of newspaper or other thin paper, as shown in diagram C. Leave one of the long edges uncut. Fold the uncut edge like a fan. Staple it together at the base and staple or glue it to the head.

4. **To make the eyes,** color eyes on the head or cut them out of colored paper and glue them on.

5. **To make the tongue,** cut out a thin strip of red felt or paper and glue it to the back of the mouth. *(continued next page)*

Diagram A

1

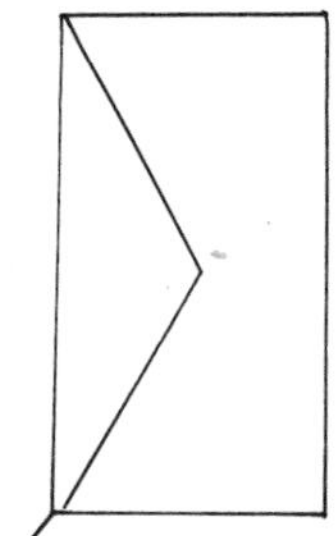

Cut off the flaps of both envelopes.

2

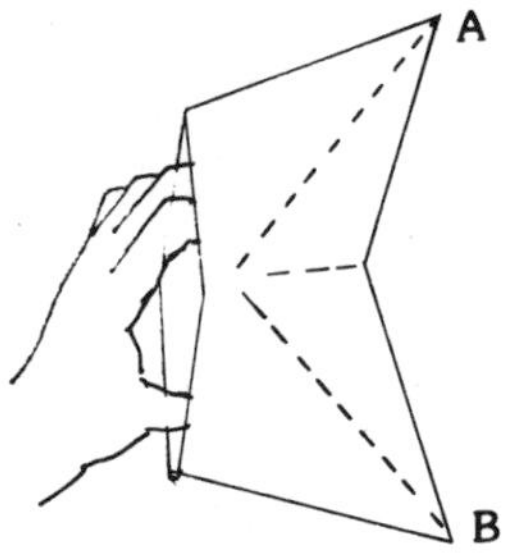

A

B

Put your hand inside the envelopes.

3

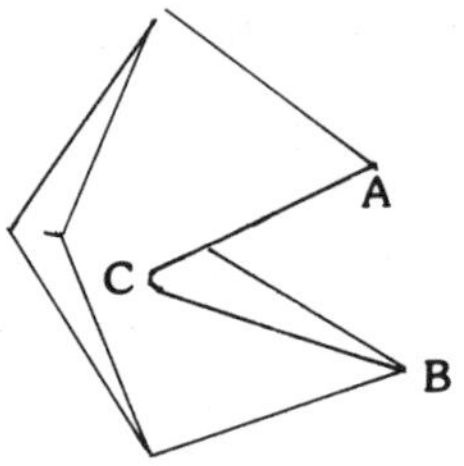

A

C

B

Push in to point C.

Diagram B

Place on fold.

D

UPPER BEAK PATTERN
(Actual size)

Glue beak here.

60

Color lower beak.

E

6. **To make the body,** draw one on construction paper and cut it out. (See the example in diagram D. The body should be about 7½″ [19 cm] long and at least 6″ [15 cm] wide.) Make feathers by cutting pieces of paper as in Step 3 and gluing them to the body in layers. (Start

Diagram C

8″

4″

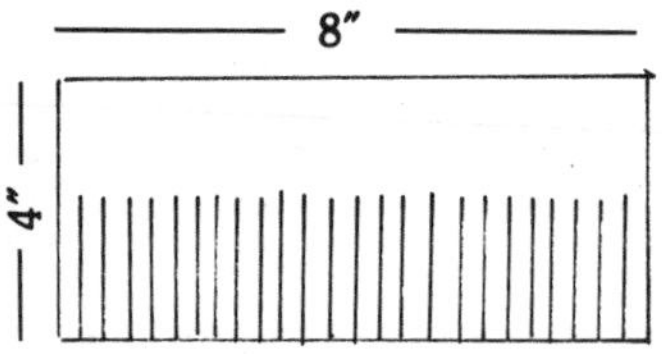

Cut strips in paper.

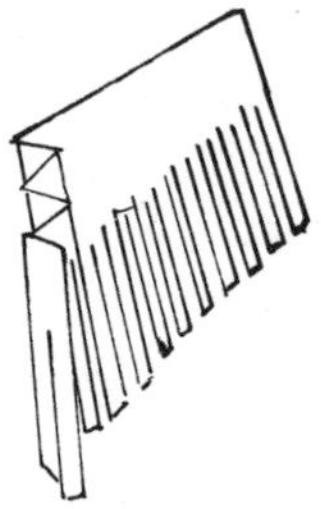

Fold like a fan.

Diagram D

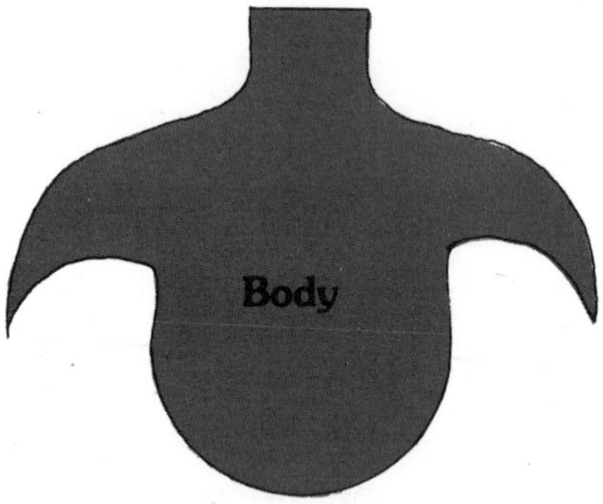

Body

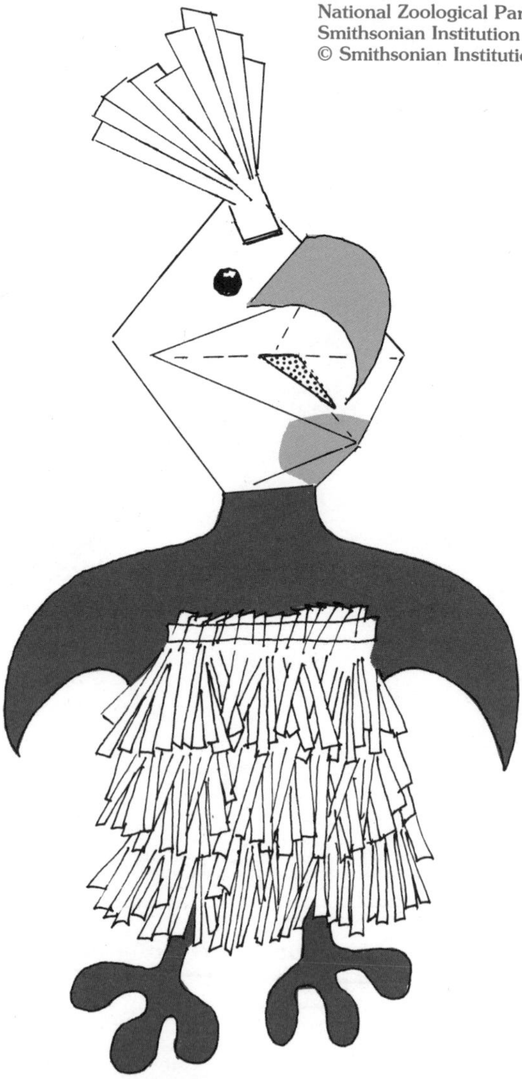

at the bottom and work up.) Add enough feathers to cover the body.

7. **To make the feet,** trace and cut out two copies of the foot pattern. Glue them to the bottom of the body.

Put your parrot puppet together by gluing the neck to the head.

National Zoological Park
Smithsonian Institution
© Smithsonian Institution

The Finished Puppet

FOOT PATTERN
(Actual size)

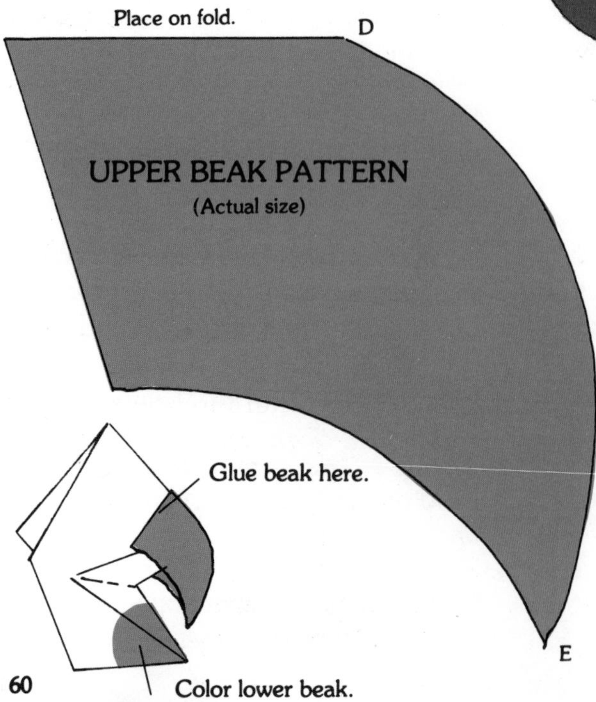

MAKE A SUET FEEDER

The loss of natural habitat is endangering many forms of wildlife. But there is one way you can help. You can provide a place where wild creatures can find food, water, and shelter to rest and raise young. This place is called a naturescape. The following pages give you some naturescaping projects.

Suet is a great source of protein for bug-eating birds, especially in wintertime when bugs are in short supply. Suet is the hard fatty tissue that surrounds the kidneys of cattle and sheep. It is usually available from your local butcher. If you can get suet, buy it in big quantities, chop it up in portions, and freeze it. If you can't get suet, make a mixture of lard and cornmeal to form a thick paste. Then add any or all of the following: peanut butter, rolled oats, crushed eggshells, or raisins. Hang the stuff by placing it in plastic netting like onions or oranges are packaged in at the grocery store. Another idea is to use hardware cloth for hanging a suet bag, or you can nail an old wire soapdish (open at the top) to a board and nail it to a tree or post and stuff the suet inside it. You can also just spread the suet on the bark of a tree.

Quick drink: Though you should try to have another water source for your naturescape, you can put a pie pan of water in your platform feeder, giving wildlife an easy opportunity for a quick drink between meals. Just be sure to keep it clean of seed hulls and other debris.

A WHIRLEY SUET FEEDER

Find a good-sized stick with branches and make a Whirley Suet Feeder. Drill or carve 1" holes above the branches. Then cut the branches back to about 3 inches, and fill the holes with suet. Screw in an eye hook, hang the feeder from a tree branch, and watch the birds go round!

Squirrels will also entertain you as they try to take advantage of the meal-o-rama.

Flowers are the perfect food for hummingbirds, but you can help during low flowering times by putting up a feeder for them.

Materials:

- small plastic soda pop bottle
- large nail
- plastic straw
- heavy string or twine
- waterproof glue
- small piece of red cardboard or plastic

INSTRUCTIONS

1. Poke a hole in the bottle about an inch from the cap. Make the hole big enough for the straw to fit.

2. Push the straw into the hole, stuffing it almost to the cap. Fill the bottle with water and hold it upside-down. Adjust the straw until the water fills it up without spilling out. Empty and dry the bottle, then glue the straw in place.

3. Wrap the string around the bottle and tie it up as shown. Make sure it is level.

4. Cut a circle of red cardboard or plastic and fit it on the straw end.

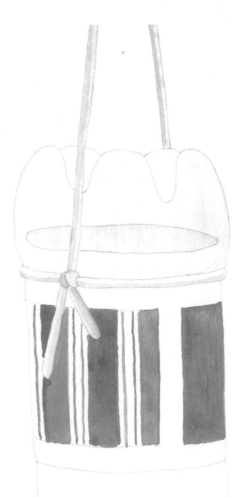

Fill the bottle with hummingbird mixture. Be careful not to squeeze the bottle. Hang it in a sunny place where hummers can find it, or even better, hang it where you have seen hummers hanging out.

There are hummingbird feed mixtures for sale, but you can make your own by mixing 1 part white granulated sugar to 4 parts water. Boil the mixture for 1 or 2 minutes. Fill the feeder and then refrigerate the leftovers. Do not use honey or artificial sweeteners, as they could make the hummers sick. And don't bother adding red food color. Just be sure there is red on the feeder. Replace the mixture every 3 days, and clean the feeder with warm water once a week.

Fruit is another food that attracts birds to your naturescape, especially in winter. You can make a "porcupine" feeder by putting an eye hook in a piece of wood and hammering long nails through the board so that they stick out the other side. Then carefully impale apple, pear, peach, and/or orange halves on the nails and hang the feeder from a tree.

Extended holiday: **Remove all the lights and ornaments and place your holiday tree outside in its stand. Redecorate it with strings of berries, raisins, nuts, fresh or dried fruit, and popcorn. Stuff suet into pinecones and nets. Birds will love the treats and the safe haven of the tree until spring. Then remove the string and the nets and add the tree to your brush pile, where it might become a nesting site.**

Another type of feeder is the hopper feeder, which uses a container to hold seed with a way to let the seeds sift out as they are eaten from the tray. This kind of design doesn't allow as many birds to visit because of its smaller size, but it is easy to make, easy to fill, and has a cover. And it gives the little birds a chance to have their own little dining area.

Materials:

- clear plastic bowl, approximately 12 inches wide
- plastic tray, such as a planter saucer, that is 3–4 inches smaller than the widest part of the bowl
- ½ pound coffee can or something similar (the hopper)
- heavy twine or other weather-resistant string
- small nail and hammer
- glue
- bottle opener and can opener
- S hook

Dirt lovers: Seed-eating birds eat dirt, sand, and small bits of rock to help in digesting food and also for mineral supplement. Since most birds don't have teeth, they need grit to chew up the seeds they eat. Grit goes into their stomachs, or gizzards, where the food they eat is ground up with help from the grit, much like the teeth in your mouth. You can set out a pan of grit, or just spread a mix in your ground feeding area. Feed stores sell ground-up shells, or you can provide your basic dirt, sand, and rocks. Put your grit in a covered area that is relatively dry. Birds might also use this area for a dustbath.

INSTRUCTIONS

1. Punch 3 holes equally spaced in the sides or the rim of the tray. Punch 3 holes equally spaced in the sides of the bowl, about 2 inches from the rim.
2. Use the bottle opener to open several double holes around the rim of the can, then remove the end of the can with the can opener.
3. Glue the can into the center of the tray (holes down), put a weight over it, and let it set overnight.
4. Cut 3 lengths of string, about 3 feet long. Tie the ends into the 3 holes in the tray. Hold the bowl upside down over the

tray so that there is about a 5-inch space between the end of the bowl and the tray. Hold each string up to the adjacent hole in the bowl, and make a large knot. Then slip the ends into the holes from the inside of the bowl, so that the knots stop the bowl from sliding down.

5. Hold the feeder up and tie the other ends of the string to the S hook. To fill the feeder, just slide the bowl up the strings. Place the feeder close to a platform feeder until birds discover it, then move it if you like.

You can also try hanging a tray with the hopper without the bowl roof. Put a plastic lid over the top of the can.

Just as food gets old and spoiled in the refrigerator, food left outside for wildlife for too long can also go bad. Clean out uneaten seed once a week in winter and every few days in warm weather, especially during wet months. Clean the feeders while you are at it. Hungry birds and other wildlife may eat spoiled or moldy food and make themselves sick.

Anting: Many birds pick up ants and tuck them under their wings and throughout their feathers, especially during the summer and fall, when they are shedding old feathers and growing new ones. Ants emit formic acid, which may act as a deterrent to lice, mites, and other annoying insects that live on a bird's body. But many birds also spread berries, cigarette butts, and other substances into their feathers. It may be that the juices emitted from ants, berries, and these other substances soothe the bird's irritated skin brought on by new feather growth. Observe carefully, and you may discover why some birds "ant!"

Piggy critters: Squirrels can be piggy when it comes to feeders. Set up a special place just for squirrels and chipmunks so your birds have a chance at their "fair share" on the other feeders. Screw two pieces of wood together like an "L." Drive a long nail through the bottom piece, fasten it to a tree, and you can impale dried corn on the cob for these furry critters. But don't be surprised if birds also find this a fun place to snack!

What kinds of bird feeders can you make? People make bird feeders out of all kinds of "throwaway" plastic and aluminum food containers. Come up with your own bird feeder and see what kinds of critters you attract!

Hide and seek: Squirrels aren't the only critters who store food away for winter. Many birds, including bluejays, will also hide food for use during hard times. They will use small holes in trees, holes they make in the ground, or anywhere else they feel is a safe hiding place. Watch them as they stuff their mouths and fly off. See if you can locate their stashes. Sometimes you will see birds steal food that they find in another's bird's stash.

BUILD A NEST BOX

Bluebird trails: For more than 50 years, bird lovers from all over the United States have been installing large numbers of nest boxes for bluebirds on country roads. Sometimes as many as several thousand nest boxes are placed one after the other on fence posts and small trees. People walk along the bluebird trails throughout the spring and summer to watch the bluebirds along with the many other birds and critters who move into the nest boxes.

Use these dimensions, or something close, for bluebirds, swallows, chickadees, wrens, small woodpeckers and other cavity-dwelling birds of similar size.

Materials:

- one piece of 1″ × 6″ cedar, 14″ long, for the back
- one piece of 1″ × 6″ cedar, 9″ long, for the front
- one piece of 1″ × 6″ cedar, 6″ long, for the bottom (cut last for correct fit)
- two pieces of 1″ × 8″ cedar, 11½″ long, for the sides
- one piece of 1″ × 8″ cedar, 9½″ long, for the roof
- 1½″ drywall screws to attach the front, (1½″ nails are okay for the rest but screws are recommended)
- two L screws for the latches
- saw
- drill
- hammer

Note: if cedar is not available, then use another type of untreated wood, 1″ thick. Untreated wood is recommended for all structures for wildlife because many paints, stains, and other wood preservatives can harm critters.

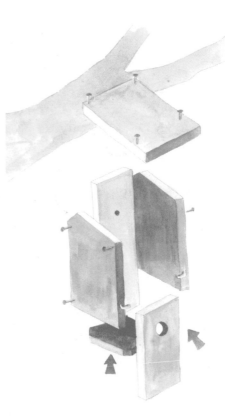

INSTRUCTIONS

1. Slant cut the sides, as shown. Cut the top corners of the sides for ventilation.
2. Cut the edges of the floor for drainage.
3. Drill a 1½″ hole, 2½″ from the top of the front.
4. Drill a small hole in the middle of the back. This will be for installation.
5. Screw the sides to the back, using four screws for each side.
6. Line up the front with the bottom of the box (leaving a ½″ gap at the top for ventilation), then screw the front to the sides, one screw each side, exactly 2″ from the top—these will be your hinges for opening the box for cleaning, so they need to be square.

BUILD A NEST BOX

7. Screw the roof to the sides, front, and back, allowing a ½″ overhang to the back.
8. Stuff the floor piece in, allowing a ¼″ space from the bottom of the sides, front, and back. Screw the floor securely from the sides.
9. Install the two L-shaped screws at the bottom on the edges of the sides. These will allow you an easy way to open the box for cleaning.

Bug-watchers: Many birds like to have a house on the edge of a clearing, such as on a tree or post that faces a pasture or garden. Most cavity-dwelling birds are insect eaters. They like to swoop and soar over the open space to gather and gulp down dinner. Watch them snap up insects as they fly through the air.

Swaying in the breeze: Some people have strung up long lines of barbed or other knotted wire between tall posts and telephone poles as a way to install their bird nest boxes. They use a wire hanger that attaches to an eye hook in the top of the nest box and hooks over the barb or knot, keeping the houses evenly spaced. Getting them up and down can be a chore, unless you make a tool to do the job. Screw a towel hook on the end of a long piece of 2″ × 2″ board to place and remove these houses. You can also use this tool for a house that is hanging from a building.

Grow your own birdhouse!

Gourds make very nice bird-houses and are popular in attracting purple martins in many areas. You can grow "birdhouse gourds" from seed, available at most seed supply houses. Gourds grow like squash, maturing in late summer in most areas. Put the gourds in a dry place and leave them until spring. Once dry, cut a 2″ hole in the wide part of the side and hollow out the dried seeds. Save the seeds for planting more gourds. Cut a few ⅛″ drainage holes in the bottom, and a ¼″ hole through the top for a knotted rope hanger. Hang it from a tree or other standing structure. It is a good idea to replace gourd houses each year, so if you don't get occupants the first season, try placing the new gourd houses in a different location the next season.

Clean-up Time!

Each fall, when you are sure all nesting is over, clean out your nest boxes. This will not only help to rid the box of bird parasites that may be in the nest, but it will give you clues as to what went on inside. Always wear gloves for this activity.

Open up the box and collect the nest materials in a box or a wheelbarrow. Make notes about what you find. Was there a nest inside? What was it made of? What did the birds use for the outside structure and the inside lining?

Bird shelves: Try a nesting shelf for birds. Birds who build nests out of mud, such as barn swallows, will sometimes appreciate a shelf to support their nests. Robins have also been known to build their nests on a shelf or windowsill. You might discover other birds who will use a shelf. Use untreated 1″ × 6″ wood, nailed together to form an "L" shape. Install the shelf on the side of a building, such as a garage or shop. If you make a bunch of them, try facing them in all directions and at different heights.

Be a nest maker

No matter what kind of nesting areas you provide in your naturescape, you can also provide nesting materials. Your butterfly "wet spot" can provide mud for mud-nest builders. But you can also offer such things as pet and human hair, bits of string, dryer lint, sticks, leaves, pieces of rags, and feathers. Hang the materials in plastic netting or hardware cloth or just put them on the ground. Make the materials available throughout the spring and summer, as many birds make more than one nest and others nest

late in the season. Observe what your nesting birds seem to like and experiment with different materials. Keep the lengths of materials at 6 inches or smaller.

Flocking for feathers: Many birds use feathers to line their nests. Feathers make the nest warm and soft for eggs and baby birds. Providing feathers, especially white ones, can attract flocks of birds during nest-building time. You can get feathers from a discarded feather pillow or comforter. You can also find feathers at a local duck pond or pet store. Or you can find out if somebody in your area raises domestic birds. They should have lots of feathers to spare!

Nests and history: **Observing the materials that a bird uses for nesting tells a story. The chipping sparrow used to be called the "hairbird" because it used horse hair to line its nest. That was back when there were more horses than cars. These days, the sparrow uses other materials for its nest, unless it is near horses! Birds that used to put snakeskins in their nests are now using cellophane instead. In most areas nowadays, bits of plastic are much easier to find than snakeskins.**

Materials:

- plastic deli-type heavy-duty container
- plastic drink bottle and lid
- small nail
- hammer
- a small bolt with a nut and rubber washer.

You can make a few of these and hang them in various locations. You can also have spare bottles available in your house so that frozen ones can be easily replaced.

INSTRUCTIONS

1. Make a hole through the bottle lid and the bottom of the container.
2. Put the bolt and washer through the plastic container, then through the lid. Fasten them together with the nut.
3. Poke a few ¼″ holes in the neck of the bottle and fill it with water.
4. Screw the bottle into the cap and hang it upside down from a tree branch or hook off a building in a sunny location. The water will drip into the plastic container only as high as the holes in the bottle.

Knee-deep: Most *nonaquatic* birds, or birds who do not normally live on the water, bathe and drink from shallow puddles or at the edges of streams. Most of them don't like to wade deeper than the height of their legs.

Hanging trays

Some birds like a hanging water source. Poke holes in the rim of an aluminum pie-pan and hang it from a tree or hook. You can also use this idea as a bird feeder.

Make a Trashcan Bath

Though just about any shallow dish can work, a metal trashcan lid turned upside down works great as a bird-bath and water tray. The gentle slope and depth of the lid is just right for nearly all sizes of birds, and the rib-bing gives them good footing. Add small pebbles to the bottom for better footing. You can place it on a pile of rocks, over a piece of clay pipe, or sink it in the ground and surround it with rocks and plants. If you are con-cerned about predators, such as cats, then it is probably best not to place any water source too close to dense shrubs. In freezing temperatures, turn the lid over to dump the ice and refill it with hot water.

A Bowl in a Bowl

You can make a combination birdbath/planter by using two bowls and sitting one inside the other. Plastic planters work well for this project, as well as other types of bowls you can find. The inside bowl is the pool and the outside bowl holds the pool in place and weights it down. Fill the outside bowl with soil and nestle the inside bowl in the middle. Put rocks and water in the inside bowl and plant flowers in the outside bowl. Place them on a tree stump or other stable surface. Then watch the birds splash and water the plants as they enjoy the bath you provided for them. You can also use gravel or sand in the outside bowl instead of soil and plants.

Shade or sun? Some critters like to bathe in the shade. Others seem to pre-fer in the sunshine. Try placing your birdbath, pool, or pond in a spot that gets morning sun and afternoon shade. Also, try putting out a few water sources in different locations, and watch what happens.

Brrr: Birds will bathe during the winter in the coldest of temperatures. Bathing helps to protect them from cold by keep-ing them free of dirt and leaving pockets of trapped air between their feathers.

Ponds

If you have room, you can make a pond! Your imagination, ingenuity, and available materials are all that you need. The bigger it is, the more critters you will invite. Any pond, small or large, will help provide water for your naturescape.

You need a place where it is okay to dig. It should be in a place you feel will be safe from predators. Have a good plan in your naturescaping notebook to get permission before you start digging or installing a pond.

The container you use for a pond can be placed on the ground or underground. If you place it on the ground, use dirt and rocks to set it in place. Some plastics do not hold up well over the years, so placing a plastic container such as a swimming pool above ground might be a good idea. If you put your container underground, measure it first and dig the hole a little wider so that you can fill back in with dirt and rocks. Let the edges sit about an inch or so above ground. Surround it with rocks and plants to make a natural looking pond. If it is deep enough, you can also try growing water plants.

Even if you have no room for a pond, just be sure you add some kind of dependable water source to your naturescape. Wildlife will appreciate your efforts.

Materials:

- a long length of rope or hose
- plastic liner such as heavy-duty garbage bags
- rocks or bricks
- shovel
- level and board for leveling

Pond-o-rama: You can use an old bathtub, a plastic swimming pool, baby tub, dish-pan or sink for a pond. Anything that holds water can work! Just be sure to allow for a variety of water depths by putting in shelves along the edges. You can make shelves out of anything that is heavy and waterproof, such as rocks and bricks.

INSTRUCTIONS

1. Use the rope or hose to lay out the pond, and try to give your pond a natural shape. It can be as small or large as you like, as long as your plan is approved. Then, start digging! Make sure the sides have a gentle slope. Pile the dirt nearby to use later for landscaping.
2. If your spot isn't already level, be sure to check as you go using the level and board. You will have to cut down from the top of the hole if your pond is not level.
3. Place the plastic liner over the hole and weight it down with the rocks or bricks. Slowly fill the pond with water.

4. Bring back the dirt you removed to create a garden. Your pond will not only provide water, but it can create some dandy little hiding spaces for frogs, toads, lizards, and other critters. Frogs like shallow mud as well as deeper areas with vegetation to lay their eggs and feed.

Water bugged: Whirligig beetles and other water bugs might find your pool or pond. Whirligigs whirl around and around on the surface and dive into the water using special paddle-shaped hairs on their legs. Their eyes are divided into two parts for seeing above and below the water at the same time. They eat small insects that fall into the water.

A gallon jug can also be used as a dripper. Poke a tiny hole in the bottom. It will stream, then drip for several hours before it needs to be refilled with water.

Dripit: Many birds like the sound of dripping water. You might install a small water-pump during nonfreezing weather to give your water source more action. If you can spare the water, just a hose trickling slowing into the birdbath or pond can attract wildlife. At this rate, you will probably use about a gallon of water an hour. In 7 hours, that is the same amount of water most people use when they flush the toilet.

FLYING DINOSAURS OR WALKING BIRDS?

There is little doubt that the earliest ancestors to the birds we see today walked and flew among the dinosaurs. Scientists find tantalizing evidence of that prehistoric world in fossil remains all over the world. But the fossil record is incomplete, and a great deal of work remains if we are ever to know what the ancient ancestors to today's birds looked like.

Can you dream of skies 150 million years ago, filled with flying creatures unlike anything alive today? They silently glided through subtropical skies and over the waves of ancient seas, hunting for fish, much like pelicans. They searched the forests and the open meadows from above, flying over the dinosaurs of the Jurassic Period, waiting for an opportunity to snatch a meal from the remains left behind by a Tyrannosaurus or another carnivore. Scientists generally agree that birds evolved from dinosaurs, or at least from a common ancestor. We also know that the earliest birds existed at the same time as flying dinosaurs, because their bones have been preserved in the same rock layers. Perhaps they even fought over the same sources of food. But how and why did early dinosaurs gradually change into birds? The fossil evidence discovered so far shows that, as the flying reptiles slowly disappeared, the variety and abundance of true birds began to increase.

There are major gaps in fossil records, missing pages of bird history that mean we have to guess about how and when birds first appeared on earth. Finding the clues to unravel this mystery is still in progress, but there is some fossil evidence

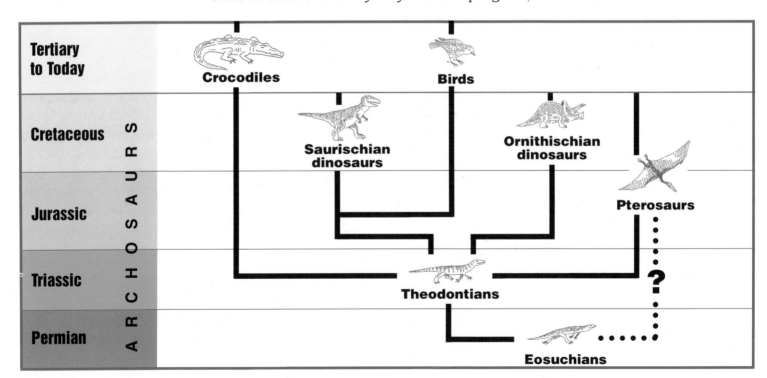

Figure 1
A common link between the birds of today and dinosaurs existed as early as 250 million years ago.

Figure 2
The fierce-looking *Preondactylus* emerged about 230 million years ago.

that can get us started. Let's look into the lives of several early birds that show the transition from prehistoric reptile to prehistoric bird.

Why Fly?

Nature experimented with the concept of flying animals at least three times over the past 200 million years, from the Triassic period to today (in reptiles, birds and bats). Birds, warm-blooded animals, proved successful in sustaining flight and evolved to fill a variety of roles in our earth's ecosystem.

Can you think of several advantages in being able to fly? How about escaping predators? It would be pretty handy to fly out of the reach of someone trying to eat you! Birds would have the advantage in searching large areas of land and water for food. They might have an element of surprise if they could attack an animal from above, rather than trying to chase it along the ground. By sleeping in trees, birds might protect themselves from the animals roaming the forest floor in search of a meal. It is suspected that these advantages helped early birds to survive, and these birds eventually became more successful at living than their reptile-like rivals.

The Fossil Record

The odds against the bones of early animals turning into fossils is very great. Conditions must be just right for fossils to form. Rapid burial in fine-grained soils and undisturbed conditions for long periods of time are just three of the critical elements of preservation needed for fossil creation and survival.

So, even though there may have been an abundance of birds in prehistoric times, the fossil evidence of birds is relatively rare. Most bones of flying birds are fragile and, because the bones are also very thin and hollow, they can be damaged easily, even if most of the conditions are met for fossil formation. The heavier bones of flightless birds fossilize more easily and, consequently, are found much more frequently. How much this influences our picture of the prehistory of birds is unknown, but it undoubtedly has had some effect on the image of the past we see in the fossil record.

Trying to locate and identify the remains of early birds involves a global search for pieces of the puzzle that help us to see how modern birds developed. Until recently, the discovery of bird fossils has been limited to developed countries in Europe and the United States. But these two areas have not provided a complete picture of the ancient world. As explorations began to search the more remote parts of the earth, other fossils came to light. Most of the important discoveries are occurring in Mongolia, specifically in the Gobi Desert. We are now beginning to close several of the gaps that blocked our understanding of bird evolution.

The Reptile Connection

Dinosaurs, possibly warm-blooded, were the probable common ancestor to both flying reptiles and birds, at least based on current evidence (see figure 1).

From what is known, it appears that nature experimented with two types of flying animals at the same time. The first experiment was with a group of reptile-like birds, called the Pterosaurs. They began to cut through the air about 230 million years ago.

One of the earliest Pterosaurs was the *Preondactylus* (see figure 2). One

Figure 3
The fossil remains
of *Pteranodon*
were found in
western Kansas,
alongside the fos-
sil remains of
early birds.

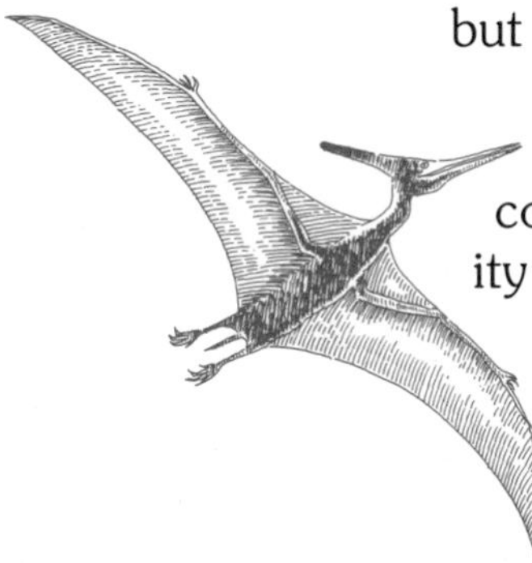

of the last was the *Pteranodon,* whose remains were discovered in the Niobrara chalk deposits of Kansas, often along with the remains of another group of flying animals that were eventually to become true birds (see figure 3). The exact point of transition from warm-blooded dinosaurs to birds remains a mystery.

The Pteranodon survived until 65 million years ago.

These flying reptiles were covered with hair. They did not have feathers but had a thin leathery membrane, attached to their arms and the sides of their bodies (see figure 4). Because the wingspan of some of these prehistoric flying reptiles was so great (23 feet for the *Pteranodon!*), they could glide for great distances. The *Pteranodon* probably relied on its ability to glide because it did not have large enough flight muscles to flap its wings continuously. In 1985, scientists built a radio-controlled model of *Pteranodon* to see how well it might fly (see figure 5). The experimental flights were successful.

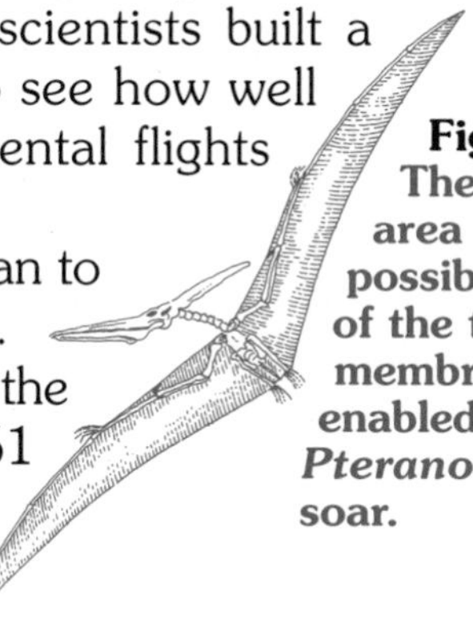

Figure 4
The shaded area shows the possible shape of the thin wing membrane that enabled the *Pteranodon* to soar.

About 150 million years ago, nature began to experiment with another type of flying animal. *Archaeopteryx* or "ancient wing," is probably the most famous bird fossil of all. Discovered in 1861 in Europe, it has been the center of controversy ever since. The discovery of *Archaeopteryx* came just two years after Charles Darwin published his famous book *Origin of the Species,* in which he presented the idea that some animals gradually evolve into different classes of animals over long periods of time. Since the "ancient wing" fossil had characteristics of both reptiles and birds, many assumed it must be the transitional animal, the so-called "missing link." Not everyone was ready to accept that idea and it touched off heated scientific debate, frequently the subject of newspaper headlines.

Many scientists consider *Archaeopteryx* a bird-like reptile, or as some scientists would call it, a "feathered dinosaur." Only eight fossil remains of this prehistoric bird are known, but a key piece of evidence was the identification of a feather impression found with skeletal remains (see figure 6).

Like true birds, *Archaeopteryx* had feathers, and its big toe was opposite of the other toes. But its bones were not hollow and it had teeth, so overall, *Archaeopteryx* has more characteristics of a dinosaur than a bird. Only the nagging presence of feathers has, for now, lumped it with birds.

But what about its ability to fly? Being able to fly would certainly make *Archaeopteryx* a bird. Wouldn't it? Not necessarily. The fossil record reveals that many reptiles were "gliders" who took advantage of small wing-like appendages and simply floated down from trees.

This raises the question of how flying began. Did birds develop the ability to fly by first climbing trees and then gliding down? Or by running and flapping their wings until they became airborne? The small fossil record of early birds doesn't tell us for sure.

Archaeopteryx probably climbed trees and then glided down to the ground. Even with feathers and wings, it probably lacked large enough muscles for a

Figure 5
Scientists experiment with a radio-controlled model of *Pteranodon,* testing its ability to fly.

powerful downstroke of its wings to enable it to run and fly.

The presence of a well-developed, keeled (like the bottom of a boat) sternum, or breastbone, is essential in birds because the flight muscles are attached to this bone, and the bone and the muscles need to be large enough to enable it to fly (figure 7). The presence or absence of the keeled sternum and the degree of development is an important feature in determining if a bird was able to support its weight in flight. The furcula, or wishbone, is also considered an important feature of true birds. The furcula is created when the two clavicles (collar bones) fuse together. The furcula is best developed in birds, as everyone knows at Thanksgiving, when we make a wish and pull on the ends our turkey's furcula, hoping to get our wish.

Figure 6
Look carefully for the feather impressions found in the fossil remains of *Archaeopteryx.*

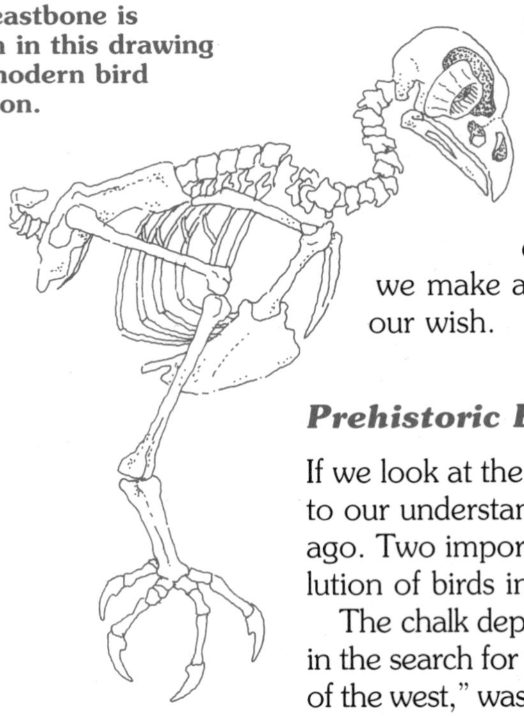

Figure 7
The keeled sternum or breastbone is shown in this drawing of a modern bird skeleton.

Prehistoric Birds of North America

If we look at the prehistoric birds of North America, the fossil records contribute to our understanding of the evolution of birds beginning about 90 million years ago. Two important discoveries made in 1870 pointed the way toward the evolution of birds in North America.

The chalk deposits of Niobrara, in west Kansas, provided important information in the search for the ancestors to our modern birds. *Hesperornis,* or the "royal bird of the west," was first unearthed in 1870. It lived approximately 90 to 75 million years ago, and its remains were found in the same rock layers where several pterosaurs were also found.

Hesperornis was flightless, but fossil evidence shows their bodies were covered with small "hair-like" feathers. The jaw also had teeth, unlike modern birds. It probably had webbed feet to help it move through the water like present-day grebes and loons. Scientists have concluded that this bird spent most of its time swimming about and diving for fish.

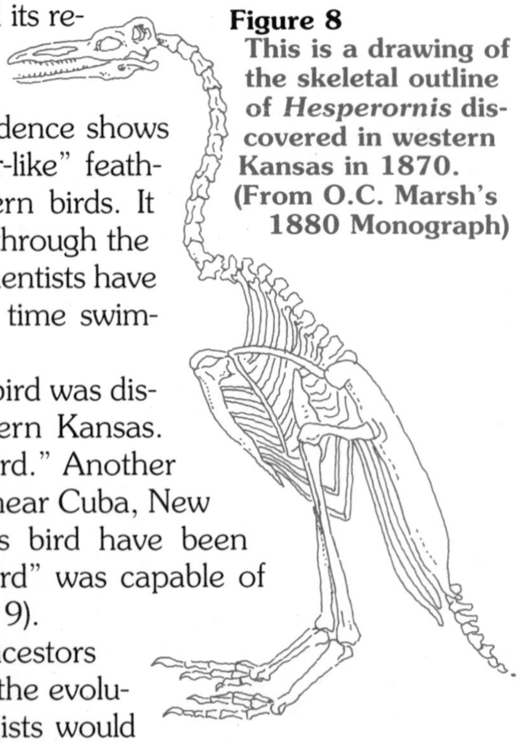

Figure 8
This is a drawing of the skeletal outline of *Hesperornis* discovered in western Kansas in 1870. (From O.C. Marsh's 1880 Monograph)

On the same expedition, another fossil bird was discovered in the same rock layers of western Kansas. This fossil was the *Ichthyornis,* or "fish bird." Another *Ichthyornis* was later discovered in 1979 near Cuba, New Mexico. Additional fossil remains of this bird have been found in Texas and Canada. The "fish bird" was capable of flight, but it, too, had teeth (figures 8 and 9).

The discovery of these two early bird ancestors filled in important missing information on the evolution of birds but, once again, paleontologists would need to rely on fossils from other locations around the world to make sense of bird development. About 65 million years ago, the earth underwent a major change in its global climate. These changes contributed to the disappearance of the reptile-like birds forever. At the same time, bird-like reptiles began to evolve into birds as we know them today.

High on the northern windswept plains of Wyoming and in northern New Mexico, the first relatively complete fossil remains of a flightless bird named *Diatryma* were found. It lived among the dinosaurs at the end of their reign and at the beginning of the age of mammals. Since those early discoveries, 50 locations in the United States, and Canada have yielded fossil evidence of this handsome ground-dwelling bird that weighed close to four hundred pounds and stood 7 feet tall. It had feathers, a large beak, and very tiny wings (see figure 10). The *Diatryma* probably survived by eating the abundant subtropical plants of the Eocene epoch, about 55 million years ago. Although lacking a "hooked beak" that would enable it to easily hunt and eat other forest dwellers as with birds of prey, it may have also scavenged on dead animals.

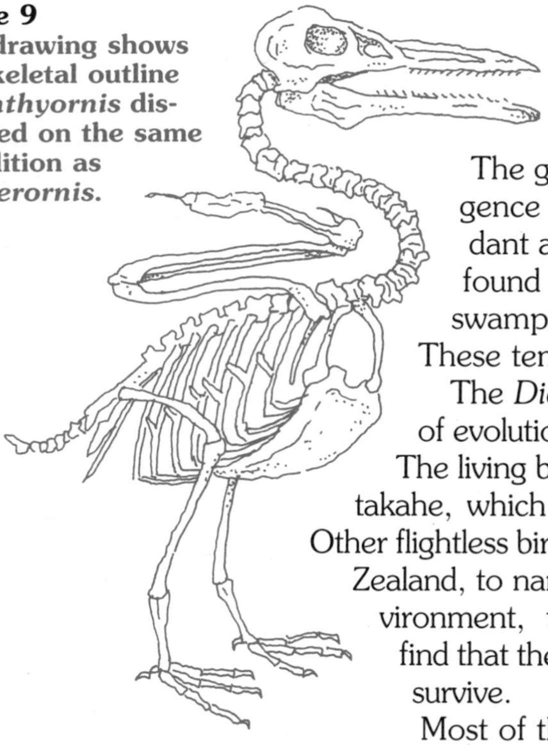

Figure 9
This drawing shows the skeletal outline of *Ichthyornis* discovered on the same expedition as *Hesperornis*.

The geologic record of the Eocene epoch shows the gradual reemergence of continents as the oceans withdrew. Volcanoes were abundant and the habitat of the *Diatryma* was varied. The plant evidence found in sedimentary rocks where *Diatryma* was found suggests swampy areas, coastal tidal zones, open grasslands, and forest edges. These temperate areas existed much further north than they do today.

The *Diatryma* represents an interesting branch on the avian (bird) tree of evolution. It remains with us today in the form of several flightless birds. The living bird species closest in structure to the *Diatryma* is New Zealand's takahe, which weighs less than 10 pounds and survives on a diet of grass. Other flightless birds include the ostrich, found in north Africa, and the kiwi of New Zealand, to name just two. Having found a successful role, or niche, in the environment, these birds did not find that they needed to fly to survive.

Most of the true bird fossils have been discovered in deposits less than 5 million years old, so our understanding of birds less than 5 million years old is much better than the rest of the fossil record. The greatest challenge and mystery is finding the missing links between the ancient birds that lived 55 million years ago and those birds that lived only 5 million years ago. Scientists are still seeking to bridge this 50-million-year gap in our understanding of bird evolution.

Figure 10
The giant flightless *Diatryma*, found in New Mexico and Wyoming lived only 55 million years ago.

FLIGHT FOR LIFE: NORTH AMERICA'S ENDANGERED BIRDS

W hat would have happened to the bald eagle if Benjamin Franklin's choice for a national symbol in 1782, the wild turkey, had appeared on official seals, coins, and dollar bills? Would anyone have noticed the eagle's absence when their numbers declined drastically in the 1960s due to the effects of the pesticide DDT? Although the wild turkey is a noble bird itself, America eagerly adopted the bald eagle as the national symbol of power and strength—a designation that probably helped protect it as early as 1940. But what about noncelebrities such as the Kirtland's warbler or the black-capped vireo? Will we miss the springtime songs of such endangered birds soon enough to save them from extinction?

Special Species

An endangered bird is any kind of bird that is in danger of *extinction,* or total loss, throughout all or a significant portion of its *range* (the places it lives, grows, eats, and reproduces). A threatened bird is one that is likely to become endangered within the near future. In all, about 250 species of waterfowl, songbirds, birds of prey, woodpeckers, parrots, and other bird species are currently endangered or threatened throughout the world-and more are being added to the "list" with alarming frequency.

Change of Pace

Living things have appeared and vanished since the beginning of life on earth. Commonly, organisms that *adapt,* or adjust, to changing conditions survive longer than others. However, human beings are draining wetlands, clearing forests, and altering other natural *habitat* (places to find food and shelter) at such a fast pace that plants and animals can't keep up with the demands. In fact, dozens of kinds of birds have become extinct in only the past 150 years due to human activities.

Going, Going, Gone

Good swimmers, great auks were common in the North Atlantic region until sailors realized that the flightless fishing birds could be herded easily onto ships to supply passengers and crew with fresh meat on long voyages. By 1844, great auks were extinct, only to be followed by the Hawaiian Sandwich rail, Carolina parakeet, and dozens more.

By the early 1900s, many bird species had suffered from overhunting and loss of habitat. In the eastern United States, it was not unusual for huge flocks of birds to pass overhead in such great numbers that the sun became blocked for hours. The passenger pigeon was such a species. Hundreds of thousands of these elegant, bluish-gray flyers would descend into lush beech and oak forests to nest or to feed on nuts and acorns. Waiting hunters shot or netted the birds by the thousands. In 1914, after the forests were logged and the birds had been sent by the trainloads to market, passenger pigeons became extinct.

Why Save A Species?

What is so important about ivory-billed woodpeckers, spotted owls, whooping cranes, California condors, and all the other threatened and endangered birds on a growing list of species?

- Each bird species is important to *biodiversity,* or the variety of living organisms on earth. At least six kinds of woodpeckers live in Florida's forests. All seem to play a similar role in their surroundings, yet each actually occupies a specific *niche* (ecological role). One case is the endangered red-cockaded woodpecker, which bores nest holes only in large living pines with heartwood disease. What is the benefit to the biosystem? Does this woodpecker promote the decomposition of the tree?

- Birds eat things that "bug" people. Songbirds consume leaf-damaging insects capable of destroying crops and forests. Efficient night hunters, owls capture mice, rats, and other rodents that can carry disease and infest buildings.

- Some birds such as hummingbirds help pollinate flowers.

- Birds bring in the bucks. Besides reducing losses to commercial crops and forests, birds help business in other ways. Each year, 65 million birdwatchers in the United States spend more than five billion dollars on binoculars, field guides, film, nesting boxes, and other related expenses. At Hawk Mountain Sanctuary in Pennsylvania, more than 50,000 visitors contribute more than four million dollars annually to the local economy.

- Some birds, such as vultures, are nature's garbage disposals. They eat the remains of dead animals.

- Birds alert us to environmental problems. For example, declines of some *migratory* birds (birds that fly from one home to another) have revealed clues about agriculture, pesticide use, and logging of tropical forests in their wintering grounds throughout Central and South America.

- Birds add to the enjoyment of life. Hearing the song of a sparrow or watching the diving of a duck can enrich and add pleasure to our lives.

Get the Lead Out

One of the first laws passed by Congress to protect North American birds was the Bald Eagle Protection Act of 1940. Raptors, or birds of prey, such as bald eagles have few natural enemies. Requiring clean water for fishing and tall trees for nests and perches, bald eagles sometimes eat *carrion* (the remains of dead animals). Viewed by ranchers as a threat to chickens, lambs, and other livestock, farmers and ranchers shot great numbers of scavenging raptors. In addition, some American Indians shot bald eagles to collect feathers for ceremonies. The Bald Eagle Protection Act suspended the decline in bald eagle numbers by making it illegal for anyone except American Indians to kill, harass, sell, or possess a bald eagle without a permit. However, many still die from accidentally eating lead shot in waterfowl and carrion.

Emergency Eggsit

Another serious threat surfaced in the 1940s, after World War II, when the use of the chemical pesticide DDT became widespread to boost agricultural production in the

81

United States. At the top of the *food chain,* birds of prey are most susceptible to the harmful chemical. DDT concentrated at each level of the food chain polluted streams, lakes, and other waterways, contaminating fish eaten by bald eagles, osprey, and brown pelicans. Peregrine falcons and eagles ate songbirds that fed on large numbers of pesticide-laden insects. The effects were disastrous.

DDT caused severe eggshell thinning in these birds of prey. Female birds laid eggs so fragile that they broke during incubation (pre-birth development usually at a warm temperature). Nests were abandoned and too few offspring were produced to sustain breeding populations. By the early 1950s, the number of bald eagles, peregrine falcons, and brown pelicans plummeted. In the early 1960s, fewer than 450 pairs of nesting bald eagles remained in the lower 48 states. A decade later, there were no peregrine falcons left east of the Mississippi River.

Road to Recovery

During this period of sudden decline, bald eagles, peregrine falcons, and brown pelicans were identified by the U.S. Fish and Wildlife Service as "endangered" birds. At the same time, the dangers of DDT became publicized in author Rachel Carson's famous book *Silent Spring.* DDT was finally banned in 1972. In 1973, the Endangered Species Act provided greater protection for all endangered or threatened animals and plants.

Nevertheless, hard work was required for these to birds recover. Although brown pelicans came back soon after chemical levels decreased in their eggs, bald eagles and peregrine falcons required special help. Scientists studied birds in the wild and collected some of their eggs for artificial incubation in research centers. The eagles and falcons could lay a second *clutch,* or group, of eggs in their nests while the others were hatched in captivity. Bird numbers began to rise when biologists *reintroduced,* or released, the young into the wild, where they would breed and produce more offspring.

Reintroduction efforts, habitat protection and improvement, and legal protections have increased the number of adult bald eagle nesting pairs to 4,500 in the lower 48 states. (Alaska has its own population of 40,000 bald eagles.) The number of American peregrine falcons is now estimated to be about 1,200 breeding pairs in the lower 48 states and Alaska. Additional birds range in Canada and Mexico. Bald eagles are no longer listed as "endangered" throughout most of the United States. Soon, the "endangered" classification of peregrine falcons will be reduced to "threatened" as well.

Return of the Condor

The number of another large predator, the California condor, was also reduced from the effects of DDT. However, condors, along with other raptors, also suffered from egg-collecting, lead poisoning, shooting, and habitat loss. These 22-pound, meat-eating birds with 10-foot wingspans once lived along the entire Pacific Coast from British Columbia to Mexico, and across to Arizona. As human populations increased, land was developed, and condors had fewer places in which to live and find food. Many condors were shot or fell ill from eating lead in other animals shot by hunters and ranchers. Some ranchers got rid of condors by poisoning the meat of dead animals that the birds ate. By the late 1930s, condors could only be found in California. The birds were nearly extinct in 1982, with only 22 individuals left.

Identified as an endangered species in 1967, California condors needed a special recovery plan. In 1987, the last wild condor was trapped to join other captive condors in a breeding program to save the species. By 1992, scientists had hatched and raised enough condors to reintroduce the birds to their natural habitat. Once a group of condors had succeeded in California, a second effort began in Arizona near Grand Canyon National Park. By late 1996, 26 California condors were flying, hunting and nesting in the wild again.

Island Birds

Hawaii is home to more endangered species than any other state. Before unique birds such as the konafinch and green solitaire became extinct, island birds were naturally protected by their special adaptations to specific food sources and habitats. When human settlement changed landscapes and introduced diseases, cats, and rats, the natural balance of living organisms was permanently altered.

For example, the ground-nesting Hawaiian goose, or nene (pronounced nay-nay), once lived between 5,000 and 8,000 feet in elevation on the slopes of many Hawaiian islands. Once numbering 25,000, the nene succumbed to hunting by introduced mammals such as dogs and pigs. In addition, grazing animals destroyed their food and shelter. Mongooses (African weasels) brought to Hawaii to kill the rapidly reproducing rats ate the nene eggs, causing populations to decline even further. At one point, fewer than 50 nene remained. The number of Hawaiian geese began to rise slowly in 1949 when restoration efforts began. Although still quite uncommon, many birds are now surviving in national parks, refuges, and zoos.

Risky Business

Today, birds become endangered from complex combinations of threats. Especially at risk are migratory birds that fly thousands of miles to countries with few environmental regulations.

About one-half of the 650 bird species that range in the United States and Canada travel to Central and South America in the winter. Flocking in North America, hundreds of thousands of birds join together to follow unseen "flight paths" each fall. Birdwatchers have noticed a significant reduction in the number of hawks and songbirds heading south each year. What is happening to these birds in their winter habitat?

- **Winter Habitat Loss**—Logging of tropical forests clears thousands of acres of trees that endangered songbirds such as the golden-cheeked warbler use for food and shelter. Some trees are sold around the world to make furniture. Most of the forest ends up on the ground where it is burned to add nutrients to the soil for crops. Migratory birds also lose winter habitat as the vast grasslands of Argentina are plowed under to plant crops or provide grazing land for cattle.

- **Pesticides**—Although DDT was banned in the United States more than 20 years ago, traces of the chemical continue to be found in North American birds. DDT and other chemicals are still used in Central and South America, where technology has not provided inexpensive alternatives.

  - 95 percent of the world's Swainson's hawks fly south to Argentina each winter, where they feast on grasshoppers that infest farmers' crops. When alfalfa was the main product, the hawks were unharmed. A shift in pesticides occurred when farmers started growing huge amounts of sunflowers for use in vegetable oil. As tractors plow the fields and apply pesticides, countless grasshoppers are stirred up. A thousand Swainson's hawks may descend at one time, receiving doses of pesticides on their feathers and eating the contaminated insects. As a result, piles of hundreds of hawks have been found dead near these crops. Five percent of North America's 450,000 Swainson's hawks are dying this way.

- Also suffering are a large number of sparrow-sized dickcissels that migrate to Venezuela and eat rice and sorghum crops. An economic burden to some growers, the yellow-breasted birds roost in the millions where these crops are grown. Farmers who fail to chase the birds away with noisemakers and firecrackers sometimes resort to poisoning pools of water where the dickcissels drink, or to spraying feeding areas with toxic pesticides before the birds arrive. Sometimes crop-dusting airplanes spray chemicals directly onto the roosting birds while they sleep at night. The outcome is the mass death of a large portion of the world's dickcissel population. Possible solutions may include finding nonlethal pest controls and paying farmers for crop losses.

- **Habitat Loss Closer to Home**—The pastimes of finding a mate, building a nest, and raising young just aren't what they used to be.

  - Bachman's warblers were once seen throughout the southern United States. A large number of these songbirds crowded into Cuba each winter, but this number declined as forests were cleared to raise sugar cane. With fewer birds left, it is now hard for the warblers to find mates when they return to the greater spaces of the United States.

  - Forests and prairie grasslands throughout the United States have become *fragmented* (broken into smaller areas) to make room for houses, crops, and grazing. Songbirds such as the least Bell's vireo, which once nested safely in the middle of dense woodlands, must now live near the forest edge where predators such as raccoons, cats, and jays eat their eggs and steal their young.

  - Smaller patches of forests, more crops of grain, and more backyard bird feeders have allowed *parasitic* (freeloading) birds to take over the nests of songbirds such as the Kirtland's warbler in Michigan. Brown-headed cowbirds sneak into warbler nests and lay eggs next to the warbler's. Unaware of the addition, warblers incubate and hatch baby cowbirds that outgrow the smaller young songbirds. Mother birds spend valuable energy producing young that will grow up only to seize the nests of other birds.

What On Earth Can We Do?

North America has a large network of wildlife refuges and national parks that allow birds to live, breed, and nest away from overhunting and development. Nevertheless, birds such as the California gnatcatcher, which lives solely in the prime real estate of coastal-sage scrub, can be saved only by local cooperation and planning. Farther from home, we need to partner with people in Central and South America to protect migratory birds. With these few important steps, it will be easier to keep common birds common than to try to rescue them once they become endangered.

APPENDIX

Questions, Questions, and More Questions

1. Birds are one group of vertebrates. What are the four others? (reptiles, amphibians, fish, and mammals)
2. Birds evolved from which group of vertebrates? (reptiles)
3. Name two characteristics that birds have in common with reptiles. (partially hollow bones, scales, similar skull and ear bones; both also lay eggs)
4. What did feathers evolve from? (reptilian scales)
5. Name two things feathers help birds do. (to fly, stay warm, attract a mate)
6. Give one reason that birds sing. (stake out a territory, defend a territory, attract a mate)
7. Name five things birds might eat. (fish, insects, seeds, nuts, nectar, aquatic plants, small mammals, other birds, dead animals)
8. True or false: Parent birds teach their young to fly. (False. Flying is an innate behavior in birds, although young birds do need to practice.)
9. Are birds warm-blooded or cold-blooded? (warm-blooded)
10. Name three things that help birds fly. (air sacs, feathers, wings, streamlined shape, light bones)
11. True or false: Birds can see color. (True)
12. Name two things that all birds need to survive. (food, water, shelter, space to mate and raise young)
13. What is preening? (the way a bird keeps its feathers clean by pulling them through its bill, nibbling them, and fluffing them out)
14. What happens when birds molt? (Their old feathers fall out and are replaced by new ones.)
15. True or false: During molting birds lose all of their feathers at once. (False. Birds lose only a few feathers at a time.)
16. True or false: The nests of some birds are built by the female alone. (True)
17. Name three ways different birds use their feet. (for swimming, climbing, running, perching, grasping, scratching)
18. True or false: Only one-third of all North American birds migrate. (True)
19. What are two things birds might use to help them find their way during migration? (sun, stars, landmarks, earth's magnetic pull, odors, sound)
20. Name three ways different birds use their beaks. (for straining, spearing, drilling, cracking, sipping, scooping, tweezing, ripping, netting)
21. Describe two ways birds defend themselves. (by flocking together, freezing in place, mobbing the predator, intimidating the predator, flying away)
22. Name two birds that have become extinct. (dodo, passenger pigeon, great auk, Labrador duck, heath hen, Carolina parakeet)
23. Describe some of the ways people have caused bird populations to decline. (by destroying habitat, overhunting, overcollecting bird parts, illegal pet trading, using lead shot, introducing new species, spraying pesticides)
24. What is a person who studies birds called? (ornithologist)
25. True or false: A bird that hatches from its egg naked, helpless, and with its eyes closed is called a precocial bird. (False. It is called an altricial bird.)
26. Name one bird that has precocial chicks. (ducks, geese, grouse, pheasants, and others)
27. True or false: Eggs must be fertilized in order to be laid. (False. Female birds can lay fertilized or unfertilized eggs but only the fertilized eggs will develop into offspring.)

Glossary

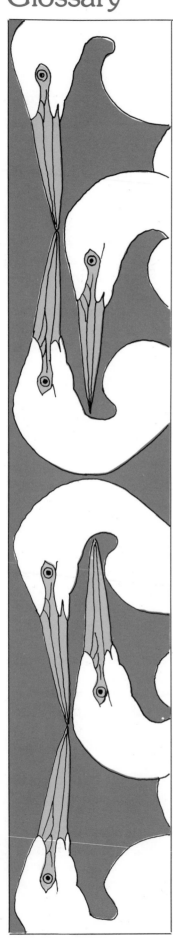

adaptation—a behavior, physical feature, or other characteristic that helps an animal survive and make the most of its habitat. For example, ducks have webbed feet that help them swim.

air sacs—special balloonlike sacs attached to the lungs of a bird that allow it to exchange gases more efficiently.

albumen—the egg white in an egg. It protects the developing embryo and is a source of the embryo's water, protein, and minerals.

altricial—birds which, upon hatching, are helpless. Most songbirds are altricial.

anting—a preening behavior in which a bird either rubs ants into its feathers with its bill or stands on an anthill and lets ants crawl through its feathers, possibly to remove parasites.

binocular vision—the act or power of focusing both eyes on a single image, thus gaining good depth perception. Birds use binocular vision when they focus straight ahead.

calls—bird vocalizations that are not songs. Calls are made during courtship, feeding, and migration, or as warnings.

camouflage—protective coloration or shape that helps hide an animal from its predators or prey.

clutch—the number of eggs laid by a female during one nesting cycle.

crop—a sac at the bottom of the esophagus in many birds that is used to store food for later digestion.

down—soft feathers next to the body that provide insulation.

egg-tooth—a small, sharp structure on a baby bird's upper mandible that helps it chip through its shell during hatching. The egg-tooth is usually lost within a week or so after the bird hatches.

fledge—to take the first flight. Birds that have just fledged are often called *fledglings*.

gizzard—the muscular part of a bird's stomach that grinds hard-to-digest food.

habitat—an animal's home. For example, the habitat of a meadowlark is a meadow.

innate—a behavior that is inherited. For example, some birds' songs are innate, which means the birds can sing them even if they have never heard them before.

migration—seasonal movement from one region to another. For example, a hawk might migrate from southern Canada to Central America for the winter.

mobbing—the attack made on a hawk, owl, or other predator by a group of birds.

molt—to shed and replace old feathers.

monocular vision—the act or power of focusing each eye independently of the other. Birds with monocular vision have a wider field of vision than those birds with binocular vision. Most birds have both binocular vision and monocular vision, depending on where they focus their eyes.

niche—the "job" of an animal or plant in its habitat. For example, the niche of a robin could be described as: daytime feeder, worm and berry eater, food for hawks, tree nester, fall and spring migrator.

ornithology—the study of birds. An *ornithologist* is a scientist who studies birds.

pectoral muscles—a bird's breast muscles. In most birds, the pectoral muscles are very powerful. They raise and lower the wings during flight.

plumage—a bird's feathers referred to collectively.

precocial—birds which, upon hatching, are completely feathered and are able to see well. Precocial birds can follow their parents and feed shortly after hatching. Ducks, geese, grouse, and most other ground-nesting birds are precocial.

preen—to clean, straighten, and fluff the feathers.

song—the notes repeated by a bird over and over in a regular pattern. Birds use song to help defend territories and sometimes attract mates.

territory—the space a bird defends from other birds (usually of the same species) for mating or feeding.

warm-blooded—being able to maintain a constant body temperature independent of the outside temperature. All birds are warm-blooded.

Birds Bibliography

Note: A * at the end of a listing indicates that a book is a good source of bird pictures.

GENERAL REFERENCE BOOKS

The Audubon Society Encyclopedia of North American Birds by John K. Terres (Wings Books, 1991)
The Atlas of Bird Migration edited by Jonathan Elphick (Random House, 1995)*
Bird by David Burnie (Knopf, 1988)*
Birding for Beginners by Sheila Buff (Lyons & Burford, 1993)
The Life of Birds 4th ed., by Joel Carl Welty and Louis Baptista (Saunders, 1988)
A Nature Company Guide: Birding by Joseph Forshaw, Steve Howell, Terence Lindsey, and Rich Stallcup (Time-Life, 1994)*

ATTRACTING BIRDS

America's Favorite Backyard Birds by Kit and George Harrison (Simon and Schuster, 1989)
The Backyard Bird Watcher by George H. Harrison (Simon and Schuster, 1988)
The Bird Garden by Stephen W. Kress (Dorling Kindersley, 1995)*
Birdscaping Your Garden: A Practical Guide to Backyard Birds and the Plants That Attract Them by George Adams (Rodale, 1994)*
The Complete Birdhouse Book by Donald and Lillian Stokes (Little, Brown, 1990)*
A Complete Guide to Bird Feeding by John V. Dennis (Knopf, 1994)
How to Attract Birds by Michael McKinley (Ortho, 1995)
Native Plants in the Creation of Backyard, Schoolyard and Park Habitat Areas by Marci Mowery (Audubon Council of Pennsylvania, 1996). Order from Audubon Council of Pennsylvania, 1104 Fernwood Ave., Ste. 300, Camp Hill, PA 17011.

FIELD GUIDES

The Audubon Society Guides to North American Birds: Eastern Region by John Bull and John Farrand (Knopf, 1977)*
The Audubon Society Guides to North American Birds: Western Region by Milkos D.F. Udvardy (Knopf, 1977)*
Birds by Herbert S. Zim and Ira N. Gabrielson (Golden Press, 1987)*
Birds is a Nature Finder bird identification wheel. By turning the wheel, information about different birds is displayed through windows. Available from Hubbard Scientific. 1-800-446-8767. All ages
Birds' Eggs by Michael Walters (Dorling Kindersley, 1994)*
Birds of the World by Colin Harrison and Alan Greensmith (Dorling Kindersley, 1993)*
A Field Guide to Eastern Birds by Roger Tory Peterson (Houghton Mifflin, 1990)*
A Field Guide to Western Birds by Roger Tory Peterson (Hougton Mifflin, 1990)*
National Geographic Society Field Guide to the Birds of North America edited by Jane McCauley (National Geographic, 1993)*
Peterson First Guides: Birds by Roger Tory Peterson (Houghton Mifflin, 1986)*
Simon and Schuster's Guide to Birds of the World edited by John Bull (Simon and Schuster, 1978)*
Spotter's Guide to Birds of North America by Dr. Phillip Burton (Usborne, 1991)*
Stokes Field Guide to Birds (two volumes: Eastern Region and Western Region) by Donald and Lillian Stokes (Little, Brown, 1996)*

CHILDREN'S BOOKS

Amazing Birds by Alexandra Parsons (Knopf, 1990). Primary and Intermediate*
Amazing Birds of Prey by Jemima Parry-Jones (Knopf, 1992). Primary and Intermediate*
Amazing Tropical Birds by Gerald Legg (Knopf, 1991). Primary and Intermediate*
Backyard Birds by Jonathan Pine (HarperCollins, 1993). Primary
Backyard Birds of Summer by Carol Lerner (Morrow, 1996). Intermediate
Backyard Birds of Winter by Carol Lerner (Morrow, 1994). Intermediate
Birds by Barbara Taylor (Dorling Kindersley, 1995). Intermediate and Advanced*
Birds and How They Live (Dorling Kindersley, 1992). Intermediate and Advanced*
The Great Bird Detective by David Elcome (Chronicle, 1995). Intermediate and Advanced
A Kid's First Book of Birdwatching by Scott Weidensaul (Running Press, 1990). Comes with cassette of bird songs. Primary and Intermediate
The Moon of the Winter Bird by Jean Craighead George (Harper, 1992). Advanced
Over 300 Fun Facts for Curious Kids: Birds (Western Publishing, 1992). Primary and Intermediate
Owl Moon by Jane Yolen (Philomel, 1987). Primary
A Year of Birds by Ashly Wolff (Puffin, 1988). Primary

AUDIO CASSETTES, FILMS, FILMSTRIPS, SLIDES, AND VIDEOS

Bullfrog Films offers bird videos, including A Celebration of Birds With Roger Tory Peterson (Advanced), which features interviews with the famous creator of bird field guides, and Songbird Story (All ages) about two friends' magical journey to learn about neotropical migrants. Call 1-800-543-3764 for a catalog.
The Cornell Lab of Ornithology offers numerous materials for educating children about birds. For teachers, there is the college-level Home Study Course in Bird Biology. Bird Notes are two-page fliers that answer often-asked questions about birds. There are 18 topics to choose from, including "Careers in Ornithology," "Providing Nest Sites for Backyard Birds," and "Landscaping for Birds." The Lab also has an extensive collection of cassettes, CDs, and videos that demonstrate bird vocalizations and behavior. And its slides and slide sets enable you to build your own collection of bird images. You can request information about these and other educational materials by writing the Cornell Laboratory of Ornithology, 159 Sapsucker Woods Rd., Ithaca, NY 14850-1999, or calling 1-607-254-2440. You can also visit their web site at http://www.ornith.cornell.edu
National Geographic Society has several bird-related titles. Bird Migration in the Americas is a 23" × 36" chart.

Birds and How They Grow is a Wonders of Learning Kit containing 30 student booklets, reproducible activity sheets, teacher's guide, and read-along cassette (Primary). *Backyard Birds* is a video for primary students. *Birds* is one of five filmstrips in the *Animals and How They Grow* set (Primary and Intermediate). *Chick Embryology* is a video for advanced students. In addition, many of National Geographic's television specials are also available on video. For catalogs and more information call 1-800-368-2728.

The Whisper of Wings teaches about endangered North American birds through music, story, and song, and features activities covering math, language arts, and science. The program comes in two levels, K-3 and 4-12, and includes teaching guide and cassette. For more information call Environmental Media at 1-800-368-3382.

GAMES AND EDUCATIONAL TOYS

Audubon's Birds of America: A Fact-Filled Coloring Book by George S. Glenn, Jr. (Running Press, 1995). Intermediate and Advanced

Birds: A Peterson Field Guide Coloring Book by Peter Alden and John Sill (Houghton Mifflin, 1982). Intermediate

Owls on Silent Wings by Ann C. Cooper (Denver Museum of Natural History, 1994). Intermediate and Advanced (children's activity book)

Shorebird Migration Game allows up to six players to assume the roles of migrating birds. Making their way around the game board teaches children the basics of migration and the importance of conservation efforts to protect the birds and their habitat. Includes all game components, English and Spanish translations, and educator's booklet. For ordering information contact the Manomet Observatory, P.O. Box 1770, Manomet, MA 02345; 1-508-224-6521.

COMPUTER AND ON-LINE RESOURCES

Discovery Channel Online features many of the Discovery Channel's and The Learning Channel's programs, including several relating to birds. A special school area for teachers contains information on how to obtain videos and other educational materials. The address is http://www.discovery.com

Journey North is an Internet-based program that engages students of all ages in a global study of wildlife migration and seasonal change. Student observations of migrating species across the country are shared with other classrooms over the Internet. Children can also follow the work of scientists who are also tracking the animals using various technologies. In past years, Journey North has followed American robins, Baltimore orioles, bald eagles, peregrine falcons, and common loons. Participation in Journey North is free; teachers need only sign up. Teachers can also purchase a packet of supplementary materials, including a 30-page teacher's guide and full-color map. For more information, call 1-612-339-6959. Or subscribe at the Journey North Internet site—http://informns.k12.mn.us/~jnorth

The Multimedia Bird Book, an interactive CD-ROM that asks Intermediate and Advanced kids to identify the calls and appearance of more than 60 birds and photograph them for inclusion in a magazine they help put together. Articles on topics from nesting to how birds fly and videos illustrating other concepts help round out the program.

Peterson Multimedia Guides: North American Birds is a CD-ROM featuring Roger Tory Peterson's guide in an interactive format. Order from Environmental Media, 1-800-368-3382.

Smithsonian Online brings the resources of the Smithsonian Institution to teachers over the Internet. By accessing the Smithsonian's Web page, teachers can find materials specifically for elementary and secondary grades, including photos that can be downloaded and reprints of articles, including "American Warblers," "The Bald Eagle: Haunts and Habitats," "Birds," and "Crane Music: A

Natural History of American Cranes." The address for the Web page is http://www.si.edu/
The National Museum of Natural History has its own Web site: http://nmnhwww.si.edu/nmnhweb.html
You can also access Smithsonian Online over America Online.

OTHER ACTIVITY SOURCES

Audubon Adventures is a classroom program featuring birds and other wildlife that includes a newspaper for kids, a teacher's guide, certificate for the class, and posters featuring wildlife habitat. It costs $35 to join for a year, which provides enough materials for 32 students. Write to National Audubon Society, 700 Broadway, New York, NY 10003 or call 1-212-979-3183.

National Migratory Bird Day Issues Pac is published by the U.S. Fish and Wildlife Service in conjunction with International Migratory Bird Day, which falls in May of each year. The Pac contains fact sheets, lesson plans, and project ideas for learning about migratory birds. To obtain youth education materials, contact the Institute for Urban Wildlife, P.O. Box 3015, Shepherdstown, WV 25443.

Partners in Paradise: Migratory Birds and Our Habitat is a curriculum for teachers of advanced students containing background information, lessons plans, and supplemental materials in a three-ring binder. For more information or to order contact the U.S. Environmental Protection Agency, 841 Chestnut Bldg., Philadelphia, PA 19107; 1-215-566-2696.

Project Feeder Watch and Project Pigeon Watch allow kids to contribute to the research of the Cornell Laboratory of Ornithology. Participants in *Project Feeder Watch* count the numbers of different species of birds that visit a home or classroom feeder. In *Project Pigeon Watch,* participants collect data on the numbers and different colors of urban pigeons. Each project comes with instructions, posters, data forms, and a quarterly subscription to the newsletter *Birdscope,* which publishes project reports. *Project Feeder Watch* costs $15 annually, and *Project Pigeon Watch* is $10 for individuals and $15 for groups. Call 1-800-843-2474 to sign up by phone, or visit their web site at http://www.ornith.cornell.edu

The Smithsonian Migratory Bird Center has several publications of interest to teachers, including some in Spanish. "Birds Over Troubled Forests" is a 32-page booklet. "Migratory Birds in Costa Rica and Panama" and "Crossroad for Migratory Birds" are bilingual booklets. *Feathered Travelers: Neotropical Migratory Birds of the Americas* is a reading and coloring book in English and Spanish. The Center also offers several free fact sheets on migratory bird conservation. For more information, contact the Center c/o The National Zoo, Washington, DC 20008. You can also visit their Web site at http://www.si.edu/natzoo/zooview/smbc/smbchome.htm

WHERE TO GET MORE INFORMATION

- county extension offices (in the phone book under local government listings)
- local Audubon Society chapters (in the white pages of your phone book)
- museums, state and local parks, zoos, nature centers
- state university departments of ornithology
- state departments of natural resources (in the phone book under government listings)

Internet Address Disclaimer

The Internet information provided here was correct, to the best of our knowledge, at the time of publication. It is important to remember, however, the dynamic nature of the Internet.

Resources that are free and publicly available one day may require a fee or restrict access the next, and the location of items may change as menus and homepages are reorganized.

Natural Resources

Ranger Rick, *published by the National Wildlife Federation, is a monthly nature magazine for elementary-age children.*

Ranger Rick magazine is an excellent source of additional information and activities on dinosaurs and many other aspects of nature, outdoor adventure, and the environment. This 48-page award-winning monthly publication of the National Wildlife Federation is packed with the highest-quality color photos, illustrations, and both fiction and nonfiction articles. All factual information in *Ranger Rick* has been checked for accuracy by experts in the field. The articles, games, puzzles, photo-stories, crafts, and other features inform as well as entertain and can easily be adapted for classroom use. To order or for more information, call 1-800-588-1650.

The EarthSavers Club provides an excellent opportunity for you and your students to join thousands of others across the country in helping to improve our environment. Sponsored by Target Stores and the National Wildlife Federation, this program provides children aged 6 to 14 and their adult leaders with free copies of the award-winning *EarthSavers* newspaper and *Activity Guide* four times during the school year, along with a leader's handbook, EarthSavers Club certificate, and membership cards. For more information on how to join, call 1-703-790-4535 or write to EarthSavers; National Wildlife Federation; 8925 Leesburg Pike; Vienna, VA 22184.

ANSWERS TO COPYCAT PAGES

FEET ARE NEAT (p.39)
1. —5, 2. —3, 3. —4, 4. —2, 5. —1.

MIGRATION MAZE (p. 38)

MOLT THE DUCK (p. 49)

1. breeding season 2. preen 3. gland 4. molt 5. fly 6. lice 7. water 8. adult 9. migrate 10. plume 11. baths 12. sun 13. down 14. birdbath 15. young; color #6—green; color #7—yellow; color #8—red; color #9—blue; color #10—brown.

BIRDBRAIN CROSSWORD (p. 58)

DOWN: 1. chicken 3. flamingo 5. robin 7. canary 9. eagle 11. raven 13. goose 15. duckling 17. feather 19. turkey
ACROSS: 2. pigeons 4. parrots 6. roadrunner 8. loon 10. nightingale 12. vulture 14. owl 16. crow 18. stork 20. dove

Index